100 FACTS

Newcastle

First published in Great Britain in 2014
by Wymer Publishing
www.wymerpublishing.co.uk
Wymer Publishing is a trading name of Wymer (UK) Ltd

ISBN 978-1-908724-16-8

Edited by John Kemp.

Typeset by Wymer.
Printed and bound by Clays, Bungay, Suffolk.

A catalogue record for this book is available from the British Library.

Cover design by Wymer.
Sketches by Becky Welton. © 2014.

Newcastle

Steve Horton

1881

NEWCASTLE EAST END'S CRICKET ORIGINS

FACT 1

In 1881 the first of two clubs who would later join together to form Newcastle United were formed in the Byker area of the city.

Stanley FC were formed in November 1881 by a cricket club of the same name, so that their members still had a sport to play in the summer. Their first match took place on 26th November against Elswick Leather Works Reserves and ended in a 5-0 victory.

The following year the name was changed to Newcastle East End, to avoid confusion with another club called Stanley in County Durham. Playing in red shirts, white shorts and black socks, they moved to a new ground in Chillingham Road and in 1889 were founder members of the Northern League, the second oldest league in the world.

Newcastle East End

first entered the FA Cup in 1890-91 and they were beaten 4-2 by Sunderland Albion in a qualifying round. The following year they reached the first round, which was the last 32 of the competition, but lost 2-1 against Nottingham Forest.

In the Northern League, Newcastle East End finished fourth, sixth and fourth in the three seasons prior to joining forces with Newcastle West End in 1892.

1886
NEWCASTLE WEST END MOVE INTO ST JAMES' PARK

FACT 2

The other club who Newcastle United derive from also had a cricket background and had been the team that played at St James' Park.

In 1882, the year after Newcastle East End were formed, Newcastle West End Cricket Club also decided to set up a football team and they initially played at Town Moor for three years. After spending 1885-86 at the Great North Road they moved to St James' Park in 1886. St James' Park had first been used for football between 1880 and 1882 by a team called Newcastle Rangers. When Newcastle West End moved in, they enclosed it by building an eight foot fence and did as much as they could to level a slope, but facilities were still basic and players had to change in local pubs.

Newcastle West End were also founder members of the Northern League in 1889 and finished runners up in the first season, only losing out on goal difference to Darlington St Augustine's. However manager Tom Watson left the club to take over at Sunderland and they struggled in the next two seasons. In 1889-90 they also entered the FA Cup for the first time, being knocked out by Grimsby Town.

By 1892 Newcastle West End were suffering from serious financial problems but with St James' Park being a better ground than Chillingham Road, they invited their great rivals Newcastle East End to join forces.

FACT 3

1892
IT COULD HAVE BEEN NEWCASTLE CITY

Newcastle East End and Newcastle West End became one club in 1892, with a number of names being suggested.

By the end of 1891-92 it was clear that the city of Newcastle could not sustain two professional clubs with Newcastle West End struggling both on and off the pitch whilst their rivals prospered.

One advantage Newcastle West End did have though was St James' Park, which was a better ground and also nearer to the city centre. In May 1892 West End invited East End to take over the lease of St James' Park as well as what remained of their assets, mainly players.

With the merger being more of a takeover, the name remained Newcastle East End and the club's first game at St James' Park was a prestige friendly on 3rd September against Scottish Cup holders Celtic, which the visitors won 1-0 in front of a crowd of 6,000.

Gates for Northern League games however remained disappointing and on 9th December a meeting of club officials and fans was held at nearby Bath Lane Hall. It was decided that to attract support from all areas of the city a new name was needed and of the suggestions - Newcastle City, Newcastle Rangers and Newcastle United, the latter was the overwhelming vote winner.

FACT 4

1893 JOINING THE FOOTBALL LEAGUE

Newcastle United joined the Football League in 1893, a year after Newcastle East End had turned down the chance to do so.

In 1892 Newcastle East End had applied to join the First Division but their application was refused, however they were invited to play in the Second Division. Due to the fact there were no big names playing there and they decided to remain in the Northern League instead.

In 1893 the newly named Newcastle United were invited to join the Second Division and this time accepted, meaning that they were joining the Football League at the same time as Liverpool and Arsenal.

Newcastle's first game was on 2nd September 1893 away to Arsenal, who were then known as Woolwich Arsenal and played in south London. It was played at the Manor Ground in Plumstead and attended by 6,000 fans. The match ended in a 2-2 draw with Thomas Crate and Jock Sorley scoring for Newcastle in the second half after they had trailed 1-0 at half time.

The following week Newcastle lost 3-1 at Burton Swifts but in their first home game they beat Woolwich Arsenal 6-0. Despite struggling early in the season when they only won two out of their first ten games, Newcastle came good from December and eventually finished fourth but this wasn't enough to be involved in the 'test matches' that decided promotion and relegation.

FACT 5

1894
THE BIRTH OF BLACK AND WHITE STRIPES

In 1894 the legendary black and white stripes were born as Newcastle United ditched the red and white that they had been playing in for the previous two years.

The club had continued to wear the red shirts and white shorts that Newcastle East End had worn, but this often caused kit clashes. Many supporters also believed that a complete break should be made from the past to ensure the support of the wider public.

At a club meeting it was decided to change to black and white stripes with blue shorts, which meant that the only time there would be a clash would be against Notts County. The change occurred during the season and it brought the team luck, as it coincided with a good run of form that saw them lose only once in four months.

There is no clear reason why black and white stripes were chosen. One theory is that the Dominican monks from a nearby friary wore black and white robes, but it is just as likely that there was a black and white strip lying around the ground and they decided to use that, as complete sets of kit were expensive. It is known that a Northumberland county side wore black and white stripes in a match at St James' Park in the late 1880s.

Whatever the reason, the shirts have remained the same ever since, with shorts changing from blue to black in the 1920s.

FACT 6

1895 A RECORD 9-0 DEFEAT

Newcastle United's record defeat came in 1894-95 when they were hammered 9-0 by Burton Wanderers in a Second Division match.

The game was played on 15th April and was Newcastle's last game of the season. They knew that whatever happened they would finish tenth out of sixteen teams and even though they were on a disappointing run and had lost seven out of nine, this result was still a massive shock.

Burton Wanderers had enjoyed a respectable first season in the Football League, after being elected the previous summer. The match at St James' Park had ended 3-1 to Newcastle but going into this game Wanderers were unbeaten in twelve.

The match was played at a ground called Derby Turn, now no longer in existence and Newcastle were already 4-0 down at half time. The normally reliable keeper W.A. Ward never played a league game for the club again.

Despite the number of goals conceded, Newcastle picked themselves up again and finished fifth the next season. Burton Wanderers on the other hand were voted out of the Football League after finishing second bottom in 1897 and four years later merged with local rivals Burton Swifts to form Burton United, who themselves folded in 1910.

FACT 7

1898
PROMOTION IN THE LAST OF THE TEST MATCHES

In 1898 Newcastle United were promoted to the First Division after they initially appeared to have lost out as the Football League stepped in to expand the top flight. Newcastle enjoyed a great season, finishing second in the league in a campaign that saw them win fourteen out of fifteen home games. They also caused an upset in the FA Cup, knocking out First Division Preston North End at their Deepdale ground.

With no automatic promotion and relegation Newcastle joined Second Division Champions Burnley as well as Blackburn and Stoke, the bottom two sides in the First Division, in a series of 'test matches' to decide who would play in the top flight the next season.

Newcastle finished third in the group of four, but controversy surrounded the last match between Stoke and Burnley. A draw would guarantee First Division football for both of them the next season and neither side had a shot at goal as they drew 0-0 although there was no proof of deliberate wrongdoing.

To settle the matter through the Football League then decided to expand the First Division to eighteen teams, meaning Newcastle were promoted and Blackburn avoided the drop. Also for the following season, the test matches were scrapped and automatic promotion and relegation introduced.

FACT 8

1901 NEWCASTLE UNITED'S FIRST INTERNATIONAL

On 18th March 1901 Newcastle United goalkeeper Matt Kingsley became the club's first international player when he appeared for England against Wales.

Kingsley was signed from Darwen in 1898 and was an ever present in his first two seasons, which included a shock FA Cup exit at non-league Southampton.

He was said to have been a character on the pitch and often waved his arms about like a windmill, preferring to punch the ball away rather than try and hold it. The England selectors were still impressed though and he was called up to face Wales in a British Home Championship match, which was played at St James' Park.

Kingsley kept a clean sheet as England won the match 6-0, with Derby's Steve Bloomer scoring four of the goals. However it would be the last time that he would be selected for England. Kingsley remained Newcastle's first choice keeper until 1903-04 when he was replaced by Jimmy Lawrence. He then moved on to West Ham United, who were then playing in the Southern League and later played for QPR, Rochdale and Barrow.

FACT 9

1901 DERBY ABANDONED

The Newcastle United v Sunderland fixture in 1900-01 was abandoned in extraordinary circumstances due to the huge numbers of spectators who had attended.

In addition to the fact that the game was a local derby scheduled for Good Friday and the added interest of both sides having title aspirations. Sunderland were top and had a nine point lead on Newcastle, but the Magpies had three games in hand and knew victory for them would really put the pressure on Sunderland.

St James' Park's 30,000 capacity was nowhere near enough for those that hoped to see the game and the terraces were full an hour before kick off, with thousands more scaling the fences and taking up position at the side of the pitch.

At 3.30pm the teams appeared and kicked off but due to continual crowd encroachment onto the pitch the referee abandoned the game within a few minutes. This led to angry scenes with some of the crowd pulling down the goalposts and fighting amongst themselves. Police reinforcements were called and several fans had to be taken to hospital.

One Sunderland fan later sued Newcastle for a refund of his entrance fee but lost the case and had to pay legal fees of £70. When the game was eventually replayed three weeks later Sunderland won 2-0 but that wasn't enough for them to win the league, with the title eventually going to Liverpool.

FACT 10

1902
STAR FORWARD LEAVES CLUB

In 1902 John Peddie, one of Newcastle United's first star centre forwards left the club after five years at St James' Park.

Often known as 'Jock', Peddie signed in November 1897 from Scottish side Third Lanark and although his debut was in the tenth game of the season against Newton Heath (now Manchester United), he still ended the season as the club's top scorer as Newcastle were promoted.

He wasn't daunted by the step up to the First Division, finishing as top scorer in the next three seasons. Despite this, he still attracted criticism from some fans, who felt that although he could dribble well and had a powerful shot he didn't move fast enough. Peddie also got into trouble with the board due to his tendency to miss games and not turn up for training. In 1900 he was suspended indefinitely but this was later lifted.

In 1901-02 Peddie managed a respectable eight goals in sixteen games, although this included two hat-tricks and he was sold to Manchester United but was only there for a year. He then moved south to Plymouth Argyle, before returning to Manchester United where he became captain. After finishing his career he emigrated to America where he died in Detroit in 1928, aged just 52.

FACT 11

1905
THE FIRST FA CUP FINAL AND BIGGEST CROWD

In 1905 Newcastle United reached the final of the FA Cup for the first time, where the biggest crowd ever to see them play saw them lose against Aston Villa.

Newcastle made a slow start to the competition, drawing 1-1 at home to Southern League Plymouth in the first round. They then made the long trek to Devon for the reply which ended in another 1-1 draw, before finally winning 2-0 in a second replay in London at Arsenal's Manor Field ground.

In the second round they needed a replay against another Southern League club, Tottenham Hotspur, winning 4-0 at St James' Park after a 1-1 draw at White Hart Lane.

As the opposition got harder, Newcastle became stronger and they beat Second Division Bolton 2-0 away in the quarter final. In the semi final at Manchester City's Hyde Road ground, they won 1-0 against fellow First Division side Sheffield Wednesday.

The final was played on 15th April at Crystal Palace against Aston Villa, who had already won the competition three times. 101,117 were in attendance with many fans clinging to trees to try and get a better view.

Despite their higher league position - Newcastle were going for a league and cup double - they couldn't overcome a Villa side who took the lead after just two minutes through Harry Hampton, who added another with fourteen minutes left to give them a 2-0 win.

FACT **12**

1905 LEAGUE CHAMPIONS

After the disappointment of losing the FA Cup final, Newcastle recovered over the next few weeks to win their first Football League First Division Championship, clinching the title with a 3-0 win at Middlesbrough in the last game of the season.

Newcastle started the season slowly, winning only four of their first nine games but seven successive wins in November and December took them to the top. However they were never able to build a commanding lead and top spot changed hands often. The situation was so tight that on 28th January a 3-2 defeat at Manchester City meant they dropped from first to fourth, with only two points separating the top six sides in the table.

A run of seven wins from eight between February and April put Newcastle in control and with just three games remaining they knew they would be champions if they could secure maximum points. However they appeared to have blown their chances following a 3-1 home defeat to Sunderland on 22nd April a week after the cup final defeat. They got away with it though as on the same day closest challengers Everton lost too, meaning Newcastle remained in control of their own destiny.

On 26th April they beat Sheffield Wednesday 3-1 at Hillsborough, and a win at Middlesbrough on the 29th would guarantee the title. A draw would be enough, providing Manchester City didn't beat Aston Villa.

Newcastle's result was rarely in doubt. Goals from Ronald Orr, Bill Appleyard and John Rutherford gave them victory as City lost at Villa, meaning Newcastle finished the season one point ahead of runners up Everton, winning the first of three titles that decade.

FACT 13

1905
ST JAMES' PARK IS BIGGEST CLUB GROUND IN ENGLAND

After becoming Champions of England for the first time, Newcastle United boasted the biggest ground in the Football League when the following season kicked off.

With Newcastle's growing stature in the game the club thought big, building a huge new stand on the Barrack Road side of the ground (now occupied by the Milburn Stand). It contained 4,680 seats with a paddock in front and even had a swimming pool for the players underneath.

On the other three sides the wooden stands were taken down and the banking expanded and properly terraced with crush barriers being fitted. Directors had visited Celtic Park and Hampden Park in Glasgow for inspiration and the total cost was £12,000.

The new look ground was opened by the Lady Mayoress on 6th September before a game with Manchester City, which was drawn 2-2. 56,000 attended a match against Sunderland the following December but even though crowds were well below capacity - 33,000 being average in 1906-07, this was still the best in the league.

Despite the new status St James' Park only remained the biggest in England for a few more years, with Everton expanding Goodison Park in 1909 to take their capacity to 69,000.

FACT 14

1907
CHAMPIONS WITH A NEAR PERFECT HOME RECORD

In their final home game of 1906-07 Newcastle United drew 0-0 with Sheffield United, meaning it prevented them ending the season with a 100% home record. However it was still enough to secure a second Football League First Division Championship in three years.

Newcastle's perfect home form meant they remained in contention for the title from the start, but the first time they hit the top of the table was after a 5-0 home win over Manchester United in early February. Eight points out of the next ten available helped them pull away from the chasing pack, but they always had to be aware of Everton who had games in hand.

On 8th April Everton slipped up when they lost 2-1 at Blackburn, meaning that Newcastle only needed one point from their remaining two games to secure the title.

On 13th April in the last game of the season at St James' Park, they clinched it in front of their fans with a goalless draw against a Sheffield United, who became the first team to avoid defeat there that season. The Blades still had a mathematical chance of winning the league themselves, although it would have needed a few rugby scores to achieve it.

The following week Newcastle lost 4-2 in their last game of the season at Bolton, but nobody was complaining. The magnificent home record meant that their points total of 51 was three more than the 1904-05 tally.

FACT 15

1909
EDWARDIAN MASTERS BEAT CLOSEST RIVALS TO WIN TITLE

When Newcastle United comfortably won their third Football League First Division Championship in 1908-09, they clinched the title with four games to spare by beating the only team with a chance of catching them.

Newcastle got off to a flying start by winning their first five games, but a run of two wins from the next six meant they were second in the table at the end of October. Their form remained inconsistent and on 5th December 1908 they were stunned when Sunderland won 9-1 at St James' Park.

That Sunderland thrashing spurred Newcastle into action and they won ten of their next eleven games. This run included a 4-0 win at Notts County on 23rd January which took them to the top of the table and from then they were never off it. On 10th April 1909 Newcastle lost 3-1 at Sunderland, their first defeat in over three months, but it only delayed the inevitable.

Two days after the Sunderland defeat second placed Everton, the only other team who had any chance of winning the league, came to St James' Park in a game which they had to win to keep their faint hopes alive. In front of 30,000 fans William McCracken scored a first half penalty and James Stewart added two in the second half to give Newcastle their third title in five years.

Such was the eventual ease of the title triumph, won by a team known as the 'Edwardian Masters' due to their attacking play, there were still four games remaining of which Newcastle won one and lost three.

FACT 16

1909 NEWCASTLE'S ONLY CHARITY SHIELD

In 1909 Newcastle United won the Charity Shield (now known as the Community Shield) for the only time in their history.

The competition was inaugurated the previous year to replace the Sheriff of London Charity Shield, which was contested between amateur and professional sides. Newcastle had won that in 1907, beating Corinthians 5-2. Whereas nowadays the winners of the Premiership and FA Cup contest the Community Shield, in its early days it was played for between the champions of the Football League and Southern League.

This meant that on 28th April 1909, two weeks after clinching the title and still with one league game left to play, Newcastle faced Northampton Town at Chelsea's Stamford Bridge ground. Goals from Stanley Allen and Jock Rutherford gave Newcastle a 2-0 victory in front of a crowd of just 7,000.

Since then Newcastle have appeared in five Charity Shields, the most recent being in 1996 when they faced Manchester United at Wembley, but have lost them all.

FACT 17

1909
11 GOAL THRILLER LOST TO LIVERPOOL

In the 1990s Newcastle United were involved in two famous games with Liverpool that both ended in a 4-3 defeat, but on 4th December 1909 the two sides played in an eleven goal classic, when Newcastle were again on the losing side.

Newcastle were reigning champions and Liverpool had only just avoided relegation the season before, but before this game Newcastle were sixth in the league, with Liverpool a place ahead of them on goal average.

Newcastle attacked Liverpool from the kick off and were 1-0 up after a minute when Liverpool keeper Sam Hardy misjudged a cross and Jimmy Howie headed into an empty net. Although Jim Stewart soon levelled, Newcastle took command and by half time Albert Shepherd had scored four times as they cruised into a 5-2 lead.

In the second half though Newcastle were shocked as Liverpool, kicking into the Kop where most of their supporters were gathered quickly pulled one back and then former Magpies player Ronald Orr struck twice to make it 5-5. The winning goal came five minutes from time from a move that was started by Orr and ended in Arthur Goddard heading in a John MacDonald cross.

FACT 18

1910
WINNING THE FA CUP AT LAST

In 1910 Newcastle completed a remarkable decade by winning their first FA Cup, finally achieving success in the competition after three final defeats.

In addition to losing the 1905 final, Newcastle also lost the finals of 1906 and 1908. The road to the 1910 final began with an away tie at Stoke City and after a 1-1 draw Newcastle then won the replay 2-1 at St James' Park. They were then drawn at home in every round, beating Fulham, Blackburn and Leicester Fosse to reach the semi finals, where they beat Swindon 2-0 at White Hart Lane.

In the final Newcastle faced Second Division Barnsley at Crystal Palace and a shock looked on the cards when the Yorkshire side took a 37th minute lead. In the second half Newcastle struggled to break down Barnsley's defence and they were frustrated when Albert Shepherd had a goal disallowed for offside. Eventually with eight minutes remaining Jock Rutherford headed the equaliser to set up a replay at Everton's Goodison Park.

At Goodison Newcastle were backed by most of the neutrals in the 60,000 crowd, as Barnsley had beaten Everton in the other semi-final. It was a much improved Newcastle performance despite being hindered by a severely waterlogged pitch and they had enough chances to be ahead at half time. The good play continued after the break and Shepherd settled the game with goals in the 52nd and 62nd minutes, the second of them a penalty after Sandy Higgins had been fouled.

The following day thousands of fans attended the homecoming at Newcastle Central Station. Newcastle were the last winners of the old design FA Cup trophy which was later presented to FA President Lord Kinnaird.

FACT 19

1911
NEWCASTLE FAIL TO WIN NEW FA CUP TROPHY

After becoming the last winners of the old style FA Cup trophy, Newcastle United couldn't win the new cup in its first season as they lost to Bradford City in the final.

Newcastle's defence of the cup began with a comfortable 6-1 home win over Bury but they were surprisingly held 1-1 at home by Northampton in the 2nd round, winning the replay 1-0. Further home ties followed against Hull, who were beaten 3-2, and Derby, a game which Newcastle won 4-0.

In the semi final Newcastle beat Chelsea 3-0 to set up a final with Bradford City. However they would have to do without leading scorer Albert Shepherd, who had scored eight goals in the competition only to injure himself in a collision with Blackburn's keeper in a league game the week before the final.

At Crystal Palace on 22nd April 1911 Shepherd's absence was notable as Newcastle enjoyed plenty of possession but couldn't convert it into chances as they also struggled with windy conditions. At the end of ninety minutes the game was goalless, meaning the sides would have to meet again at Old Trafford the following Wednesday.

In front of 58,000 fans with an estimated 20,000 locked out Newcastle fell behind after fifteen minutes when keeper Jimmy Lawrence uncharacteristically helped a Jimmy Speirs header into the net. Despite enjoying plenty of possession for the rest of the game Newcastle couldn't find an equaliser with their forwards appearing nervous in front of goal.

It meant that Bradford were presented with the new FA Cup trophy, which is still in use today and had ironically been made by Bradford jewellers Fattorini & Sons.

FACT 20

1916 VICTORIA CROSS FOR DONALD BELL

In the First World War Donald Bell, who had played for Newcastle United's reserves in 1911-12, was awarded the Victoria Cross for his bravery in the Battle of the Somme.

Originally from Harrogate, Bell joined Newcastle in the summer of 1911 from Crystal Palace but failed to establish himself due to strong competition for right back places. He never made a first team appearance and is only known to have played five games for the reserves.

In 1912 he returned to his native Harrogate where he became a teacher, but also signed for Second Division Bradford Park Avenue, establishing himself in the side in 1913-14.

When the First World War broke out he joined the West Yorkshire regiment, becoming the first professional footballer to enlist and he rose to the rank of Second Lieutenant. On 5th July 1916 at Horseshoe Trench he braved heavy fire to attack and destroy an enemy machine gun, saving the lives of many of his soldiers. Just five days later he was killed carrying out a similar act of bravery.

Bell's posthumous Victoria Cross was presented to his widow Rhoda by King George V and it is now on display in the National Football Museum in Manchester.

FACT 21

1922 RECORD APPEARANCE HOLDER'S LAST GAME

At the end of 1921-22 Jimmy Lawrence, who has played more games for Newcastle United than any other player, finally ended his career after eighteen years at St James' Park.

Goalkeeper Lawrence was born in Glasgow in 1895 and joined Newcastle in 1904 from Hibernian where he had not been first choice. He made his Newcastle debut in a 2-0 win over Manchester City on 1st October 1904 and played in all but one of the remaining 28 games that season as they won the title.

Lawrence's consistency was an important factor as Newcastle won two more league titles that decade and also reached five FA Cup finals in seven seasons, winning one of them.

If it hadn't been for the First World War, which saw the Football League suspended for four years, he would have played far more than his total of 498 games for the club. However, he still remains the holder of Newcastle's record number of appearances although he surprisingly was only once picked by Scotland, for a game against England at Goodison Park in 1911.

After seeing off several other keepers to remain the number one, Lawrence finally lost his place in 1921-22 to Bill Bradley and his last game was a 2-1 home defeat to Bradford City on 14th April 1922. He then went into management with South Shields, who were then a Football League club, as well as Preston North End and German side Karlsruhe.

FACT 22

1924 FIRST TRIP TO WEMBLEY

In 1924 Newcastle beat Aston Villa to win the FA Cup in what was only the second final to be played at Wembley.

Newcastle beat Portsmouth in the first round but then needed four attempts to overcome Derby, eventually winning 5-3 after three 2-2 draws. They then won 1-0 at Watford in the third round before hammering Liverpool 5-0 at St James' Park in the quarter final. In the semi final Manchester City were beaten 2-0 at Birmingham's St

Andrew's ground with Neil Harris getting both the goals. To avoid a repeat of the chaotic scenes the previous year when an estimated 200,000 gained admission through flimsy barriers and spilled onto the pitch before kick off, the 1924 FA Cup final was made all ticket and a crowd of 91,695 attended.

Most of the game was played in torrential rain and for an hour the sides were evenly matched. However as the game drew to a close Newcastle's superior stamina showed and with seven minutes left Harris pounced to score during a goalmouth scramble to put them 1-0 up. Two minutes later as Villa chased an equaliser Stan Seymour broke clear and fired a low shot past the keeper to confirm Newcastle's victory.

It was Newcastle's second FA Cup victory and programmes for the match are perhaps the rarest to obtain of any from Wembley finals. Due to the heavy rain and the fact much of the stadium was uncovered, many fans used them to keep dry and few survived. Collectors have paid as much as £6,000 at auctions in recent years.

FACT 23

1925
NEWCASTLE FACE HARTLEPOOL

The only time that Newcastle have faced fellow North East side Hartlepools in a competitive game was in the third round of the FA Cup in 1924-25.

The match against a side that was then known as Hartlepools United took place at St James' Park on 10th January 1925. Newcastle were overwhelming favourites going into the game, lying fifth in the table while their opponents were third from bottom of the Third Division North.

Despite the time of year it was a fine day and 35,000 fans turned out to see Hartlepools put up a good fight for the first half, when they tested Bill Bradley with a couple of long shots. It wasn't until the 40th minute that Newcastle found a breakthrough when Neil Harris headed in a Stan Seymour cross.

Newcastle started the second half better and they made the game safe before the hour with goals from Tom McDonald and Willie Cowan. Roddie McKenzie added a fourth with fourteen minutes remaining before Hartlepools replied with a late consolation.

The win over Hartlepools didn't put Newcastle on the road to Wembley however, as they were beaten by Leicester in the next round. The Foxes won 1-0 in a replay at Filbert Street after the sides had drawn 2-2 at St James' Park.

FACT 24

1925
HUGHIE GALLACHER ARRIVES

In December 1925 Hughie Gallacher, Newcastle United's most prolific ever centre forward, signed for the club.

Newcastle signed the 22 year old forward from Airdrie, where he had scored 91 goals over the previous four seasons helping them to three second place finishes and their first Scottish Cup success.

The £6,500 fee was a huge amount for the time but Gallacher showed his worth on his debut against Everton on 12th December, scoring two goals in a 3-3 draw. He ended that season with 21 league goals from only nineteen appearances, then the following season was appointed captain and scored 36 times as Newcastle won the Football League First Division Championship for the first time since 1909.

As well as his success on the pitch, Gallacher attracted plenty of headlines off it, being arrested for fighting on the High Level Bridge and leaving his wife for the seventeen year old daughter of the owner of one of his local pubs. He also pushed a referee into the bath, which led to a two month ban from the Football Association and was not afraid of voicing his opinions of teammates that he felt were not performing.

Prior to his transfer to Chelsea in 1929, which sparked angry scenes amongst fans, he scored 143 goals in 174 appearances, a strike rate of 82% that no other Newcastle striker has matched.

Gallacher eventually settled on Tyneside after his career was over but his life came to a tragic end in 1957. Faced with a court appearance concerning an assault on his son, he committed suicide at Low Fell in Gateshead by jumping in front of a train.

FACT 25

1927 NEWCASTLE'S OLDEST PLAYER

When Newcastle United lost 2-0 at Birmingham on 9th April 1947 Billy Hampson made his last appearance for the club at the age of 42 years and 226 days.

Hampson had signed from Norwich in January 1914 but the outbreak of the First World War interrupted his Newcastle career and he guested for Leeds City between 1916 and 1919. When the Football League resumed for 1919-20 he was 37 years old but he still had to wait his chance at right back due to the form of Bill McCracken, who he finally dislodged from the side in 1923.

He went on to become the regular right back for the next three seasons, playing in the 1924 FA Cup final. In 1926-27 he lost his place to Alf Maitland but remained at the club, coming in for two games in April when Maitland was unavailable. The first was a 6-1 win against Arsenal at St James' Park, then three days later he was part of the side that lost to Birmingham 2-0 at St Andrew's.

Hampson left Newcastle the following September but continued playing for South Shields in the Third Division North, finally retiring in 1930 just a few months before his 48th birthday. He then went into management with Carlisle and Leeds, moving into scouting after the Second World War.

He died in 1966 aged 83 and it is unlikely that any outfield player of his age will ever play for Newcastle again.

FACT 26

1927 CHAMPIONS FOR FIRST TIME IN 18 YEARS

In 1926-27 Newcastle won their fourth Football League First Division Championship, with Hughie Gallacher's record 36 goal haul being a major factor in the success.

After finishing tenth in 1925-26 Newcastle didn't make a spectacular start to the new season, winning only three of their first nine games, meaning they were ninth in the table at the start of October. But they went on a run of eight wins from the next ten and after going top following a 1-0 over Leeds at St James' Park on New Year's Day they were never off it.

Easter was to be a crucial time in the title race, when Newcastle faced one of their closest challengers Huddersfield twice in five days. On 15th April (Good Friday) Newcastle beat them 1-0 at St James' Park then the following day they won 3-2 against Tottenham in another home game. This meant that victory over Huddersfield on 19th April at their old Leeds Road ground would secure the title, but Newcastle lost 1-0, keeping the Yorkshire club's slim hopes alive.

The title was finally wrapped up in the second to last match against Sheffield Wednesday at St James' Park. Gallacher scored both the goals in a 2-1 win, taking his personal goals tally to 36 in the league for the season, a record that has not been matched by any Newcastle player since.

FACT 27

1930
THE 1ST DIVISION'S FIRST PLAYER MANAGER

In 1930 Andy Cunningham became player manager of Newcastle United, the first appointment of its kind in the top flight. He was also arguably Newcastle's first manager in the modern sense of the word.

After nearly 400 appearances for Rangers in the Scottish League, where he averaged nearly a goal every other game, Cunningham moved to Newcastle and made his debut on 2nd February 1929 against Leicester at the age of 38. At the time he was the oldest debutant in the Football League.

In January 1930 Cunningham was appointed the player manager, the first time a top division club had made such an appointment. He played in only five matches whilst also being manager, the last an FA Cup fifth round tie against Brighton.

Prior to Cunningham's appointment Frank Watt, who had been secretary since 1895 was effectively the manager, although officially the club was ran by a committee. Watt though did not pick the team and Cunningham became the first individual at the club to have total control over player selection.

Cunningham led Newcastle to an FA Cup triumph in 1932, but he left the club in 1935 a year after relegation. He then returned to Scotland where he managed Dundee and became a sports writer.

FACT 28

1930 ST JAMES' PARK'S RECORD CROWD

The highest attendance at St James' Park was on 3rd September 1930 when 68,386 squeezed in to see Chelsea.

At first glance, the fact Newcastle's record crowd occurred at this time in the club's history and against Chelsea is surprising. The Magpies had only avoided relegation by one point the previous season and lost the opening game of the new campaign. Chelsea were not the most high quality of opposition and were nowhere near as a big a draw as other big sides of the time such as Arsenal or Everton.

In addition the match was a midweek fixture and it was the height of the Great Depression, times of severe economic hardship. However in Chelsea's line-up there was one player who the supporters wanted to see and were prepared to make sure they spared the money to do so. Ex-Newcastle striker Hughie Gallacher was returning to St James' Park for the first time since being sold to the London club in controversial circumstances the previous year.

It was a measure of Gallacher's popularity that more than a year after he left, such a big crowd turned up to see him and his all round performance didn't disappoint. However his teammates failed to raise themselves to his level and were guilty of some poor finishing.

In the second half Newcastle were reduced to ten men when Jimmy Nelson went off injured, but they didn't let this get them down and Jackie Cape scored the only goal of the game. With many obstacles to overcome to expand St James' Park further, the record crowd looks safe for many years to come.

FACT 29

1932 THE OVER THE LINE FA CUP FINAL

When Newcastle beat Arsenal 2-1 to win the FA Cup in 1931-32 there was controversy over their first goal when the referee allowed the game to continue after the ball appeared to have gone out of play.

Newcastle needed replays to win their third and fourth round ties against Blackpool and Southport, the latter of which were beaten 9-0 at St James' Park after a 1-1 draw at Haig Avenue. Home wins over Leicester and Watford in the next two rounds followed before Chelsea were beaten 2-1 in the semi final at Huddersfield.

At Wembley, Bob John headed Arsenal into a fifteenth minute lead but the controversial equaliser came seven minutes before half time. Jimmy Boyd's low cross from the right was fired into the net from the edge of the six yard box by Jack Allen. Despite protests from Arsenal's players the goal stood, although had they played to the whistle they may have managed to stop Allen as some defenders stopped believing the referee must have seen the ball go out. Film replays later showed that the ball had in fact crossed the line by at least a foot.

Buoyed by their good fortune, Newcastle dominated the rest of the half and had two good efforts saved by the keeper. After the break they remained in control and were by far the better side, the winning goal coming from Allen in the 72nd minute when he shook off three challenges before scoring with a cool finish.

It was Newcastle's third FA Cup success and afterwards they were presented with the trophy by King George V.

FACT **30**

1934
LATE SLUMP LEADS TO RELEGATION

After 35 years in the First Division, Newcastle were relegated in 1933-34, only entering the drop zone in the final three weeks of the season following an alarming slump in form.

The season didn't start well, winning only one of their first ten games. However with six of the games being draws and only two points being given for a win, it was enough to keep them out of the bottom two places.

Despite results being inconsistent, good home form kept them out of imminent danger and they didn't lose at St James' Park until Everton beat them 2-1 on Christmas Day. Amazingly the next day they played the same opposition at Goodison Park and secured a 7-3 victory, and on New Year's Day thrashed Liverpool 9-2 at home.

On 3rd February Newcastle won 2-1 at Birmingham to go twelfth in the table, seven points clear of Sheffield United who occupied 21st place. However they then went twelve without a win, including a 4-0 defeat at Sheffield United, slipping into the bottom two in their third from last game, a 4-1 loss at Huddersfield.

In the final home game Newcastle beat Wolves 5-1 to climb out of the relegation zone, but 21st place Chelsea were a point behind with three games to play, compared to Newcastle's one. On 23rd April Chelsea's win over Leicester meant Newcastle were back in the relegation zone and they knew failure to beat Stoke in their last game of the season would condemn them to the drop.

At the Victoria Ground, Newcastle went down 2-1, meaning that the following season they would be playing Second Division football for the first time since 1898.

FACT 31

1938 RELEGATION AVOIDED ON GOAL AVERAGE

The closest Newcastle United ever came to playing in English football's third tier came in 1938 when they only avoided falling to the Third Division North on goal average.

Since relegation Newcastle had finished 6th, 8th and 4th but started 1937-38 very poorly, winning only one of their first eleven games meaning they were second bottom in the middle of October. However a run of six wins from eight games lifted them away from danger and they were fourteenth at Christmas.

In the New Year the improved form continued and a 3-1 win at Stockport on 2nd March lifted Newcastle into tenth, with games in hand on all but one of the teams below them. However a run of just one win in the next nine took them perilously close to the drop zone with four games remaining. Stockport were adrift at the bottom, but the next six sides were separated by just one point so Newcastle's sixteenth place wasn't as safe as may have seemed.

On 21st April Newcastle had a crucial 3-1 home win over Chesterfield, but lost 2-0 away to the same opposition two days later. They then lost the penultimate game of the season 2-0 at Swansea, leaving them in seventeenth just one point ahead of the relegation zone.

The way the fixtures had been generated was on Newcastle's side however. Although they were away to Luton in their last game two of the teams below them, Barnsley and Nottingham Forest were playing each other. Newcastle's superior goal average meant they could only be relegated if that game was a draw and they lost 9-0.

In the end Barnsley and Forest drew 2-2 but Newcastle's 4-1 defeat ensured survival.

FACT 32

1946
NEW SIGNING'S DOUBLE HAT TRICK IN 13-0 WIN

On 6th October 1946 Newcastle's new signing immediately set about repaying his transfer fee when he scored six goals in a record club victory.

A few days before this game Len Shackleton had been signed from fellow Second Division side Bradford Park Avenue for £13,000, the same fee Newcastle had received from Liverpool for Albert Stubbins the previous month.

Although Newcastle were third in the table and Newport had lost 7-2 at home the week before, nobody could have foreseen the astonishing events that would take place that afternoon. It took Shackleton just five minutes to make an impact, setting up Charlie Wayman for the opening goal. He then lobbed the keeper for his first goal, the first of four he scored in a six minute spell. Wayman then got two to complete his hat-trick and make it 7-0 at half time.

In the second half Shackleton got two more and Wayman took his tally to four, while Jackie Milburn scored twice and Roy Bentley got one. The victory remains a joint English league record, but ironically later in the season Newport, who finished bottom of the table and were relegated, won the return game 4-2 at their Somerton Park ground.

The *Sunday Sun* reporter had described Shackleton's display as "masterly" but although he scored 25 goals in 57 league games he was sold to Sunderland fifteen months later for a British record fee of £20,500. He was often accused of playing for himself rather than the team and the board didn't like his tendency for practical jokes. He became a far more legendary player on Wearside than Tyneside, having once said of Newcastle "I don't care who beats them."

FACT 33

1940
WILLIE MALEY'S RETIREMENT

February 1940 finally saw the retirement of Willie Maley, who had managed the club for an incredible 43 years.

Maley had been just 29 when he was appointed as secretary-manager in 1897. For the first decade of the club's existence they had bought a lot of players but Maley set about a policy of developing young talent, which paid off when the club won six successive league titles between 1905 and 1910.

Another successful period followed when four titles were won between 1914 and 1917, which included the 62 game unbeaten league sequence. His third great team, which included Jimmy McGrory, tasted league success in 1936 and 1938 and won the Scottish Cup in 1937.

Maley also pioneered foreign tours and in addition to managing Celtic he did a lot of charity work and owned the Bank restaurant in Queen Street, where board meetings were held and players often attended before and after matches.

Sadly Maley's management of the club ended in disappointment. Ill health had forced him to miss much of the 1938-39 season and after the outbreak of the Second World War Scottish football was organised on regional lines.

After fourteen matches of 1939-40 Celtic were bottom of the Western Division and he was persuaded by the Board to retire, the decision was announced in the match programme for the game with Morton on 10th February.

Despite the extraordinary length of Maley's time in charge, it is not a world record. West Bromwich Albion's Fred Everiss was in the post 45 years from 1902 to 1947 and at Auxerre in France, Guy Roux was manager from 1961 to 2005, a total of 44 years.

FACT 34

1945 CUP WIN ON CORNERS

In 1945 Celtic were presented with the Victory Cup for winning a charity match to celebrate VE Day, the result of it having been decided on corners.

VE Day marked the end of the Second World War in Europe due to the surrender of Germany. 8th and 9th May were declared public holidays and the committee who organised the Glasgow Charity Cup quickly proposed to hold a match between Celtic and Rangers to raise money for charity, with a cup to be presented to the winners.

However Rangers declined to take part as they were preparing for the final of the Southern League Cup against Motherwell three days later. As such Queen's Park stepped in to play the match which was held at Hampden Park.

Johnny Paton scored the Celts goal in the game which ended in a 1-1 draw but with no time for a replay the cup was awarded to Celtic on the basis they had won one more corner during the match.

The cup that Celtic were presented with has the inscription 'Presented by the Glasgow Charity Cup Committee to Commemorate Victory in Europe 1945. Match at Hampden Park Celtic v Queen's Park Won by Celtic FC.'

FACT 35

1947
WORLD'S BEST SUPPORTED SECOND DIVISION CLUB

In 1946-47 Newcastle United became the first club in the world to attract one million fans through the turnstiles in a single season. This statistic is made even more remarkable by the fact Newcastle were in the Second Division and failed to gain promotion.

Football crowds were booming across the country as the Football League resumed for the first time in seven years after being suspended during the Second World War and men were demobbed from the army. The first home game of the season, against Swansea, attracted a crowd of 54,966 while the next home game after the 13-0 demolition of Newport, against fellow promotion hopefuls Manchester City on 19th October, attracted a huge 65,798.

60,000+ crowds were also recorded for games against Burnley and Tottenham, the latter match occurring on 18th January and ending in a 1-0 win for Newcastle.

Generally speaking most crowds were between 45,000 and 55,000, extremely good considering it was one the worst winters on record and much of St James' Park was not under cover. From Christmas onwards Newcastle were outside the top two promotion places but crowds only fell below 40,000 for the last three games during May when promotion was beyond them.

The following season, when Newcastle were promoted, crowds got even better and the average of 56,299 remained a record until Manchester United bettered it in 1967-68.

FACT **36**

1948 RECORD FRIENDLY ATTENDANCE

When Newcastle took on Liverpool in a friendly on 14th February 1948 the game was watched by a record friendly crowd.

The match was arranged as it was FA Cup fifth round day and both sides had been knocked out, Newcastle losing in the fourth round against holders Charlton. It gave fans a chance to see former crowd favourite Albert Stubbins at St James' Park again, playing for a team who were now the First Division champions against Newcastle's new star man Joe Harvey.

Newcastle were second in the Second Division but unfortunately they were no match for the Reds, who won 3-0 thanks to goals from Billy Liddell, Kevin Baron and Willie Fagan. Stubbins, who was Reds captain for the day also missed a penalty but this didn't stop news reports describing the opposition as a 'Liverpool Machine' who gave Newcastle 'a football lesson in teamwork, polish and finishing.'

The attendance was 44,830 and remains the largest for a friendly match played in England between two English sides, although it has been bettered for friendlies and testimonials between English and foreign opposition.

FACT 37

1948 PROMOTION HERO BREAKS ARM

After missing out on promotion in 1946-47 Newcastle United went up a year later but there was bad luck for the player who got the goals that sealed the return to the First Division.

Newcastle gave notice of their intentions when they hammered Plymouth 6-1 at St James' Park in the opening game of the season, although before Christmas they were mainly third in the table behind pacesetters Birmingham and West Bromwich Albion. However on Boxing Day Newcastle won 1-0 against West Brom at The Hawthorns and then beat them 3-1 at St James' Park on New Year's Day to move above them into second. Newcastle slipped to third again at the end of February but they had a game in hand on second place Cardiff, who they went back above over Easter.

On 17th April Newcastle played third place Sheffield Wednesday at home, knowing that a win would be enough to secure promotion barring freak results in their last two games. They looked to be heading to victory only for Wednesday to equalise with eight minutes remaining. Then Frank Houghton, a 22 year old forward who hadn't scored in any of his previous twelve games for the club, struck in the last three minutes to send the crowd of 66,483 wild. Unfortunately for Houghton he broke his arm scoring the second, one of several injuries that blighted his Newcastle career.

There were two hallmarks to the promotion season. One was consistency, as Newcastle never went more than two games without a win and were always there or thereabouts whilst other teams such as Cardiff,

Southampton and West Brom faded away. The other was the magnificent home form in front of a record average crowd which resulted in eighteen home wins out of 21, with an incredible 72 goals being scored.

FACT 38 — 1949 NEWCASTLE'S TEN MATCH TOUR

One of Newcastle United 's most exhaustive trips abroad was in the summer of 1949 when they went on a month long tour of North America.

Following promotion from the Second Division Newcastle had done extremely well in their first season back in the top flight, running eventual champions Portsmouth close before finally finishing fourth.

They then set sail on a six day voyage aboard the Queen Mary, for their ten game trek which took them from the Atlantic to the Pacific coast and back, playing their first game on 19th May in Montreal and finishing exactly one month later in New York.

Captained by Joe Harvey Newcastle scored 79 goals in their ten games with Jackie Milburn, who turned down the chance of representing England on a tour of Scandinavia, getting 31 of those. Newcastle hit double figures on three occasions, winning 13-2 against Saskatoon, 16-1 against Edmonton and 11-1 against Washington All Stars.

The closest game against local opposition was a 7-4 win against Winnipeg on 6th June, then the final two matches were against Swedish side Kamraterna, who were beaten 4-0 in Toronto and 3-0 in New York.

In 2005 a complete set of tour programmes was put up for auction in Nottingham, with bids being invited of over £1,000.

FACT 39

1950 NEWCASTLE'S FIRST WORLD CUP PLAYER

The first Newcastle United player to appear in a World Cup match didn't appear for England or one of the other home countries but instead Chile.

Jorge (George) Robledo was born to a Chilean father and English mother in Iqueque in 1926. At the age of five his family moved to West Yorkshire and after he left school he initially worked as a miner and played part time for Huddersfield before joining Barnsley on a full time basis.

George and his brother Eduardo (Ted) signed for Newcastle in January 1949 for a combined fee of £26,500, although Ted took longer to establish himself in the side and had only been signed to ensure George agreed to the deal. George soon endeared himself to Newcastle fans when he scored his first goal for the club in a 2-1 win over Sunderland.

After eleven goals in thirty games in 1949-50 George was called up to the Chilean World Cup squad, despite hardly speaking a word of Spanish. He was the only player in the sixteen teams at that World Cup to play his football in a different country to what he represented.

George's first game was a 2-0 defeat to England, who had Newcastle team mate Jackie Milburn in their squad. Chile were then beaten 2-0 by Spain but George did score in a 5-2 victory over the USA.

George and Ted continued playing for Newcastle until 1953 when they left for Colo Colo in Chile, where George was top scorer two seasons running. George's total of 82 league goals for Newcastle was an English record for a non British Isles player until Dwight Yorke overtook it half a century later.

FACT 40

1951 NEWCASTLE ROCK BLACKPOOL TO WIN FA CUP

Newcastle won the 1950-51 FA Cup, beating a Blackpool side that were hot favourites and had one of the game's favourite players in their side.

Blackpool had finished third in the league with Newcastle fourth so a close contest was anticipated. However, most neutrals favoured Blackpool because their team contained 37 year old England international Stanley Matthews, a player who often added thousands to the gate wherever he played.

Matthews was a constant threat down the wing in the first half, but so often Blackpool's other forwards didn't take advantage of the crosses he provided. At the other end Newcastle were frustrated by Blackpool's offside tactics, which frustrated centre forward Jackie Milburn for most of the first half.

In the fortieth minute Newcastle did take the lead and ironically it was one of Matthews' mazy dribbles that led to it. Once again he crossed but Blackpool's forwards were not in the right position and the ball was cleared. From the centre circle the ball then broke loose to Milburn who ran forward and calmly slotted the ball past the keeper to complete his record of scoring in every round.

Newcastle's second goal came in the 55th minute and had no good fortune attached. It came about after a brilliant move that ended with Ernie Taylor backheeling the ball to Milburn who drove it home from thirty yards for one of the great cup final goals.

There was no way back for Blackpool after that goal as Newcastle won the FA Cup for the first time in twenty years.

FACT 41

1952 SECOND SUCCESSIVE FA CUP WIN

In 1951-52 Newcastle repeated their FA Cup success of a year earlier, becoming the first team to retain the trophy in the 20th Century.

Newcastle beat Aston Villa, Tottenham, Swansea, Portsmouth and Blackburn to reach Wembley, where their opponents were Arsenal. This meant that the final was being contested by the previous two winners of the trophy.

Newcastle were underdogs having finished ninth in the league compared to Arsenal's third. However the Gunners were dealt a blow after 35 minutes when they were reduced to ten men after Wally Barnes was forced to go off with a twisted knee. In the second half further injuries to Arsenal players meant that they had only seven fully fit men on the field.

Given the circumstances, Arsenal were never going to make an entertaining game of it and dug in to do all they could to frustrate Newcastle. Their captain Joe Mercer, the oldest player on the field aged 37, was their best player and an inspiration with his tackling.

However Arsenal were eventually undone by the brilliance of Scottish international Bobby Mitchell, who had on one occasion showed some amazing trickery in a run that saw him beat four players before his shot was blocked. With five minutes left he crossed from the left and George Robledo headed in from six yards to put Newcastle ahead.

Newcastle's victory meant that they had now won the FA Cup five times and they had become the first team to win the trophy two years running since Blackburn Rovers in 1890 and 1891.

FACT 42

1952
THE HIGHEST SCORING SEASON

As well as winning the FA Cup in 1951-52 Newcastle scored 98 league goals, their most in a single season but it was only enough to finish eighth in the table.

Newcastle showed their attacking prowess on the opening day of the season when they beat Stoke 6-1 at St James' Park. After losing their next home game 1-0 to Bolton they hit seven in their next two, beating Tottenham 7-2 and Burnley 7-1.

After losing 1-0 at home to Fulham on 29th September, Newcastle scored in every one of their next nineteen games, the run eventually coming to an end in a 3-0 defeat at Wolves on 16th February. In their next game things returned to normal as Huddersfield were beaten 6-1 at home, a result that meant Newcastle were fifth in the table six points behind leaders Manchester United. At this stage they had scored 81 goals, an average of 2.6 per game and looked well on their way to scoring over 100 goals.

From then on, perhaps distracted by the FA Cup run, Newcastle's form slipped and they won only one of the next eight games, failing to score in three of them.

Any hopes of scoring 100 goals looked to be ended in the second to last game, a 4-1 home defeat by West Bromwich Albion which left them on 92. However against Aston Villa on the last day of they season they looked on target to reach it as they led 4-1 at half time. In the second half though they could only add two more, but the final total of 98 was still impressive and has never been matched by any Newcastle side.

FACT 43

1953 FLOODLIGHTS SWITCH ON

When St James' Park's first floodlights were installed in 1953 spectators were still left in the dark when they were turned off at half time.

Newcastle were one of the first club's to install lights, which could still only be used for friendlies as their use hadn't been approved for competitive matches. They consisted of eight poles, each topped with five lights and their novelty meant a crowd of 41,000 attended the switch on for a friendly with Celtic on 25th February 1953. It was a keenly contested and physical game despite its friendly status and Newcastle took the lead after 29 minutes when Jackie Milburn set up George Robledo to score. However they were glad to be in the lead at half time given Celtic's forward Willie Fernie had missed four good chances.

The crowd, which included a large number of Celtic fans keen to see their team take on the English FA Cup holders, were surprised at half time when the lights were turned off to save electricity. Each of the forty bulbs had a strength of 1,000 watts, sixteen times as powerful as an average household bulb.

Thirteen minutes into the second half Robledo added another after he had again taken a pass from Milburn, but Celtic were disappointed to lose when they felt three penalty claims were dismissed.

The fairly basic floodlight system lasted only five years, being replaced in 1958 at the cost of £40,000 after the FA and Football League had allowed competitive matches to be played under them.

FACT 44

1955
GEORDIES BEAT GAUDIES WITH FASTEST FINAL GOAL

Newcastle won their third FA Cup in five years in 1954-55, beating Manchester City 3-1 in game that saw Jackie Milburn score the fastest cup final goal at that time.

Newcastle beat Plymouth, Brentford, Nottingham Forest and Huddersfield to reach the semi-finals against Third Division York City. The underdogs came close to an upset at Hillsborough, cancelling out Vic Keeble's opening goal to force a replay at Roker Park where Newcastle made no mistake, winning 2-0.

At Wembley, Manchester City walked out of the tunnel wearing track suits over their kits, something unheard of at the time, leading to some terming them the Gaudies. Newcastle, firmly focused on the game and took just 45 seconds to score when Milburn headed in a corner.

City's cause wasn't helped when defender Jimmy Meadows went off injured midway through the half, having been given a torrid time by Newcastle winger Bobby Mitchell. However they didn't give up and Bobby Johnstone equalised a minute before half time.

Newcastle took the game to City in the second half and they had control of the game before the hour mark. In the 53rd minute Mitchell drove the ball home when the defence failed to clear properly and four minutes later he turned provider, crossing for George Hannah who scored after City keeper Bert Trautmann failed to hold the ball.

Milburn's goal remained the fastest in FA Cup final history until Roberto Di Matteo scored after 42 seconds for Chelsea against Middlesbrough in 1997. In 2009 Everton's Louis Saha broke that record again, taking just 25 seconds to score against Chelsea.

FACT **45**

1955
THE FIRST FLOODLIT FA CUP TIE

Newcastle were involved in more FA Cup history in 1955 when St James' Park hosted the first tie under floodlits, although the game involved two other clubs.

At that time unlimited replays were played to determine ties, with the second replay being held at a neutral ground. This meant that after Darlington and Carlisle drew 0-0 at both their Feethams and Brunton Park grounds, St James' Park was chosen to host the third game of this first round tie.

The game was played on the evening of 28th November 1955 in front of 35,000 fans, a huge crowd for a match between two Third Division North teams.

Only two points separated the sides in the league table, an indication of why the first two games had been so close. However on this occasion Darlington were by far the better side and inspired by former Newcastle player Ron Greener, they won 3-1 to set up a second round tie with Accrington.

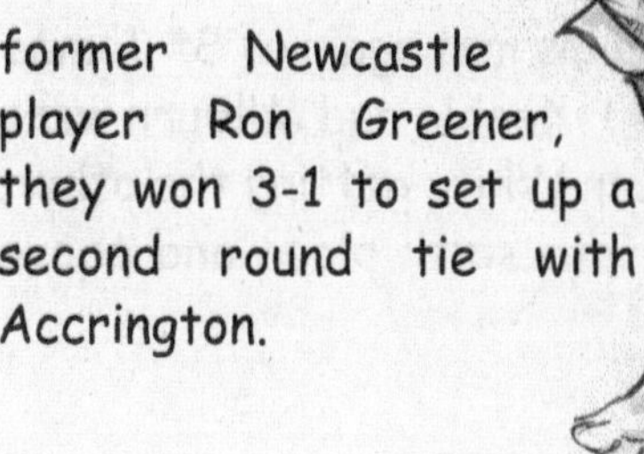

FACT 46 — 1955 BOXING DAY DEMOLITION OF SUNDERLAND

Newcastle United's biggest win over Sunderland came on Boxing Day 1955 when they thrashed them 6-1 in front of over 55,000 fans at Roker Park.

Newcastle were having an inconsistent season and going into the match were in eleventh place, having drawn only three of their 23 games. Sunderland were in fifth, but had suffered some heavy defeats, losing 8-2 at Luton and 7-3 at Blackpool so the potential was there for a big Newcastle win if the right side showed up.

On Christmas Eve Newcastle had beaten Preston 5-0 at St James' Park and they continued where they left off, racing into a 3-0 lead in the first eighteen minutes thanks to goals from Vic Keeble, Jackie Milburn and Bill Curry. Keeble got his second after 28 minutes and the score remained 4-0 until half time.

Three minutes into the second half Sunderland got a goal back but it was not to be the start of a fightback, as Milburn made it 5-1 midway through the half. In the 81st minute Curry got his second and Newcastle's sixth to complete the rout.

The following day the teams met again at St James' Park with Newcastle winning 3-1. Keeble and Milburn were again on the scoresheet, with Len White getting the other. This result lifted Newcastle into sixth place and above Sunderland in the table.

FACT 47

1957 JACKIE MILBURN RETIRES

At the end of 1956-57 Jackie Milburn, Newcastle United's leading league goalscorer, left the club.

Known as 'Wor Jackie' and with the full name of John Edward Thomas Milburn, he joined Newcastle during the Second World War and began his career as a right winger, although he was able to play anywhere across the forward line and took over the number nine shirt after Charlie Wayman left the club in October 1947.

He scored twenty goals in 39 appearances as Newcastle were promoted in 1947-48 and for the next four seasons scored at least a goal every other game in the First Division. Able to turn in a tight space and with a powerful shot, he scored both goals in the 1951 FA Cup final and the opening goal when Newcastle won the trophy in 1955.

Milburn was 33 when he left the club at the end of 1956-57 to become player manager of Linfield, where he was top scorer two seasons running and won the Irish League. After a brief spell as manager of Ipswich in 1963-64 he returned to

Tyneside where he became a journalist for the News of the World.

Such was the devotion to him on Tyneside that when a testimonial was held for him ten years after he left the club, 45,404 turned out to see an all star match that included his cousins Bobby and Jack Charlton and legendary Hungarian Ferenc Puskas.

Milburn's total of 202 goals for Newcastle was eventually bettered by Alan Shearer, but Shearer was never able to equal his 177 league goals. He died in 1988 of lung cancer and 30,000 lined the streets for his funeral. His legacy lives on with the Milburn Stand at St James' Park being named after him and a statue of him standing in the shadow of the stadium at Strawberry Place.

FACT **48**

1958 STAN SEYMOUR LEAVES

After spending nearly thirty years in different roles at Newcastle United, Stan Seymour stepped down as team manager at the end of the 1957-58 season.

Seymour was refused a contract by the club as a teenager due to his small size, but after playing for Bradford City and Greenock Morton he was back at St James' Park in 1920. A pacey left winger, he also had an eye for goal and scored 73 times in 266 appearances, including in the 1924 FA Cup final.

After leaving the club in 1929 he ran a sports shop but in 1938 was invited to become a director, with the directors' committee again having a hand in team selection.

As head of the committee, Seymour had control of first team affairs and he was effectively team manager for the FA Cup wins of 1951 and 1952. He had also given Jackie Milburn a trial in 1943 and when Duggie Livingstone, who had been appointed team manager in 1954, tried to drop Milburn for the 1955 final Seymour stepped in to overrule him. Seymour believed that the manager's job was primarily to train and motivate the players but not actually pick the team.

Seymour became team manager again in 1956, but after only avoiding relegation on goal average in 1958, Charlie Mitten was appointed to the role. Seymour would remain on the board though until his death in 1978.

FACT 49

1961
TWO GOALS A GAME BUT STILL RELEGATED

In 1960-61 Newcastle were relegated to the Second Division despite scoring 86 goals.

They had finished eighth in 1959-60 and won their opening two fixtures, beating Preston 3-2 away then hammering Fulham 7-2 at St James' Park.

However although finding the net was easy enough, Newcastle struggled in defence. Over the course of the season they kept a clean sheet in only three of their 42 games and had some high scoring matches, including a 5-5 home draw with West Ham.

Their total of 86 goals scored was more than second placed Sheffield Wednesday managed, but the 109 conceded was the worst in the division - bottom club Preston let in only 71. It meant Newcastle's matches saw a total of 195 goals scored, an average of 4.64 a game although this still wasn't the highest - Chelsea scored 98 and conceded 100 for an average of 4.71.

In the first half of the season Newcastle didn't really look in danger, but a run of eleven games without a win between December and February dragged them towards the relegation zone. With three games remaining Newcastle were third from bottom and their fate was in their own hands, but they lost 2-1 at bottom club Blackpool who then climbed above them in the table.

With Newcastle having played one more game than Blackpool, they now needed a miracle to stay up. Despite winning their last two games 4-1 at home to Bolton and 4-2 away to Blackburn, Blackpool got the point they needed on the last day to send Newcastle down.

1965

FACT 50 NEWCASTLE WIN PROMOTION DENTING RIVALS HOPES

After a four year absence Newcastle United went back up to the First Division in 1964-65, a 2-0 win over fellow contenders Bolton on Good Friday being enough to confirm promotion.

Newcastle began the season well and lost only one of their first nine games, against Northampton who would also be promoted with them. Although successive defeats to Plymouth and Ipswich saw them drop to third they were never out of the two promotion places after 24th October, when they beat Crystal Palace 2-0 at St James' Park.

Highlights of the season included a 5-0 home win over Northampton on 12th December, part of a seven match winning run that also saw Newcastle beat Middlesbrough twice over Christmas. A key factor in the success was an excellent home record, with just one of 21 games being lost.

On Good Friday Bolton, who were in third place and trailed Newcastle by seven points, came to St James' Park. In front of a huge crowd of 59,960, goals from Jim Iley and Willie Penman gave Newcastle a 2-0 win to secure promotion with three games still to play. While the fans celebrated, the players had to make the trek to South London where they drew 1-1 with Selhurst Park the following day, before journeying to the North West to take on Bolton on the Monday.

By then Bolton's chances of going up had ended after they could only draw at Rotherham on the Saturday. Newcastle drew 1-1 at Burnden Park to put them within touching distance of the Championship, which was secured on 24th April with a 0-0 draw against Manchester City at St James' Park.

FACT 51

1968
TENTH PLACE FINISH GOOD ENOUGH FOR EUROPE

In 1967-68 Newcastle secured their place in European competition for the first time, despite finishing in mid-table. They enjoyed a steady first half of the season and were sixth at Christmas. They maintained this good form for the first two months of 1968 but after a 2-0 win against Wolves on 24th February kept them in fifth, they only won one of their last twelve games.

Their last two matches were against the two Manchester clubs who were vying for the title. Their penultimate game was lost 6-0 against Manchester United at Old Trafford, then a week later Manchester City won 4-3 at St James' Park to win the league. Newcastle finished tenth, having lost more games than they won and closer in points to relegation than the fifth place they occupied less than two months earlier.

However, due to a unique set of circumstances involving the clubs above them Newcastle qualified for Europe for the first time. Second place Manchester United won the European Cup, which they would defend the following season. Liverpool (third), Everton (fifth) and Chelsea (sixth) should have gone into the Fairs Cup, for which fourth place Leeds had qualified as League Cup winners.

However an unusual rule regarding the Fairs Cup, the forerunner of the UEFA Cup and Europa League, meant that only one club per city could enter. This barred Everton from taking part. Moving down the table the same rule prevented Tottenham (seventh) and Arsenal (ninth) competing. West Bromwich Albion, who had finished eighth, qualified for the Cup Winners Cup as FA Cup winners, leaving Newcastle to enter the Fairs Cup.

FACT 52

1969
FIRST AWAY WIN BRINGS EUROPEAN TRIUMPH

Newcastle's first season in Europe saw them victorious in the final of the Fairs Cup, which was eventually completed in the middle of June.

After beating Feyenoord 4-2 on aggregate in the first round (4-0 at home and 0-2 away), Newcastle faced Iberian opposition for the next three rounds, in which they eliminated Sporting Lisbon, Real Zaragoza and Vitoria Setubal.

After beating Setubal, Newcastle had to wait almost two months to play the semi final, which was an all-British affair with Rangers. After a 0-0 draw at Ibrox, Newcastle won 2-0 at St James' Park in a match that was marred by violence by Rangers fans.

The first leg of the final was played at St James' Park in front of 60,000 fans a week later. In the second half two goals from Bobby Moncur and another from Jim Scott gave Newcastle a commanding 3-0 lead.

In the second leg at the Megyeri Uti Stadium in Budapest, Newcastle were totally outplayed in the first half and could easily have been more than 2-0 down at the break. However a crucial away goal in the first minute of the second half by Moncur meant that Ujpest now needed three goals to win and four minutes later Preben Arentoft made it 2-2. Ujpest were totally deflated and Alan Foggon, who had come on as a substitute just a minute earlier, scored a third goal in the 74th minute.

The win in Budapest was Newcastle's first away win in Europe that season and had been witnessed by only a few hundred supporters due to travel restrictions imposed by the Communist authorities. It also remains the last time that the club have won a major trophy.

FACT 53

1970 AN ALL ENGLISH EUROPEAN TIE

The only time that Newcastle have faced another English side in European competition was in 1969-70 when they knocked Southampton out of the Fairs Cup on away goals.

Newcastle started their defence of the trophy by beating Dundee United 3-1 on aggregate, then Portuguese side Porto in the second round, winning 1-0 at home after drawing 0-0 away. In the third round they were drawn against Southampton, who like Newcastle had eliminated Portuguese opposition in the previous round, winning 8-4 on aggregate against Guimaraes.

The first leg was at St James' Park on 17th December 1969, much of it during a snowfall. A well drilled Southampton defence held on for a 0-0 draw, the first time Newcastle had failed to score at home in Europe. It could have been worse for the Magpies as Willie McFaul had to make a great save from Ron Davies in a one on one situation.

Before the return leg took place the two sides met in the FA Cup at The Dell on 3rd January, Southampton winning 3-0. The following Saturday they were due to face each other again in the league at St James' Park but this was postponed due to the weather.

The Fairs Cup second leg tie took place on 14th January. Southampton dominated from the start, Mick Channon scoring in the twentieth minute. McFaul was brilliant in goal however and kept the Saints from further scoring. Then with just six minutes left Bryan 'Pop' Robson equalised during a goalmouth scramble. There was still time for Southampton to fight back but McFaul was again on hand to deny them, taking Newcastle through on away goals.

However in the quarter final Newcastle went out on away goals themselves. They beat Anderlecht 3-1 at home but lost 2-0 away.

FACT 54

1971
SUPERMAC ARRIVES

In the summer of 1971 Malcolm Macdonald arrived at Newcastle United and instantly wrote himself into local folklore with a hat trick against Liverpool on his home debut.

Newcastle paid Second Division Luton £185,000 for the 21 year old, a hefty sum at the time as they sought to secure a striker who could be idolised in the way Hughie Gallacher and Jackie Milburn had been.

In the first two games of 1971-72, both away from

home, Newcastle failed to score and then in their first home game were up against Liverpool, whose defence had set a new record for least goals conceded the previous season, letting in just 24.

After Emlyn Hughes had given Liverpool the lead Macdonald equalised from the penalty spot and then put Newcastle 2-1 up with an unstoppable shot from the left hand corner of the box. Before half time Liverpool had a chance to level the scores but Willie McFaul saved a penalty from Tommy Smith.

In the second half Macdonald completed his hat trick when he held off the challenge of Alec Lindsay to slide the ball past Ray Clemence and although Kevin Keegan pulled a goal back for Liverpool they couldn't find an equaliser.

That season Macdonald played in every league game, scoring 23 goals. He went on to become Newcastle's fifth leading scorer of all time and maintained an average of a goal every other game until he was sold to Arsenal in 1976, a move that was hugely unpopular with fans.

FACT 55 — 1973 NEWCASTLE WIN ANGLO-ITALIAN CUP

In 1973 Newcastle were the last winners of the Anglo-Italian Cup, a short lived competition between English and Italian sides.

The first Anglo-Italian Cup was organised in 1970 to provide some consolation to Swindon Town, who had won the League Cup but were denied entry to European competition by UEFA as they were a Third Division side. Entry was open to any club who wasn't playing in Europe and teams were split into two groups of eight, which consisted of four sides from each country.

Newcastle won all four of their group games against Roma, Bologna, Como and Torino to set up a semi final with Crystal Palace, the best ranking English side in the other group. After a 0-0 draw at Selhurst Park on 11th May, Newcastle won the return leg 5-1 at St James' Park ten days later.

The final against Fiorentina was played as a one off match in Florence on 3rd June before 45,000 fans. Newcastle went ahead thanks to an own goal by Superchi in the 35th minute and on the hour David Craig added a second. Fiorentina pulled one back with ten minutes remaining but Newcastle held on for victory.

Due to the general lack of interest in the competition it was abandoned after that season and re-established in 1976 for non league clubs. In 1992 it was re-born for second tier clubs but it failed to inspire either players or fans and Newcastle failed to win any of their group games in the one season they took part.

FACT 56

1974 BRENDAN IS NEWCASTLE'S ONLY WEMBLEY WINNER

The FA Cup final of 1974 was one to forget for Newcastle United fans as they saw their team outclassed by Liverpool, meaning athlete Brendan Foster was the only thing they had cheered all day.

Newcastle initially made hard work of reaching the final, drawing 1-1 at home to non league Hendon in the third round before winning the replay 4-0. They again stuttered against lesser opposition in the fourth round, as Scunthorpe snatched a 1-1 draw at St James' Park, before Newcastle won the replay 3-0.

In the fifth round West Bromwich Albion were beaten 3-0 at The Hawthorns then in a controversial sixth round game Newcastle beat Nottingham Forest 4-3 at St James' Park. However the game had been delayed due to a pitch invasion while Forest led 3-1 and the FA ordered a re-match at Everton's Goodison Park. That was drawn 0-0 then Newcastle won the replay at the same ground 1-0. In the semi final at Hillsborough, Malcolm Macdonald scored both goals in a 2-0 win over Burnley.

Before the match at Wembley a 3,000 metre challenge race took place involving Foster, who was world record holder over two miles, and Finland's Juha Väätäinen, the 5,000 and 10,000 metre European champion. Foster, wearing a black and white striped vest, won the race to the cheers of 35,000 Newcastle fans. Sadly it turned out to be all they had to shout about that day, as a hugely disappointing Newcastle side were outplayed by Liverpool, who cruised to a 3-0 victory.

FACT 57

1974 NEWCASTLE RETAIN TEXACO CUP

In 1974-75 Newcastle United won the short lived Texaco Cup for the second year running, meaning they were the only team to win the competition twice.

The competition began in 1971 and was open to sixteen teams from England, Scotland, Northern Ireland and the Republic of Ireland who hadn't qualified for European competition. Sponsored by petrol giant Texaco, £100,000 prize money was available, a considerable sum at the time. Newcastle entered for the first time in 1971-72, reaching the semi finals where they were beaten by Derby. The following season they were knocked out at the same stage by Ipswich.

For the 1973-74 competition only English and Scottish teams took part.

Newcastle beat Morton then Birmingham to reach the semi finals, where they faced Dundee United. After losing 2-0 at Tannadice, Newcastle overturned the deficit by winning the home leg 4-1 in front of a crowd of just 5,009. The final against Burnley generated much more enthusiasm and 34,450 turned up at St James' Park to see Newcastle win a one off game 2-1 thanks to goals from Malcolm Macdonald and Bobby Moncur.

In 1974-75 teams were split into four groups of four for the first stage. Newcastle topped a group that also included Carlisle, Middlesbrough and Sunderland and then had aggregate 4-3 and 5-2 victories over Aberdeen and Birmingham in the quarter and semi finals. Unlike the previous year the final was a two legged affair and after a 1-0 defeat against Southampton at The Dell, Newcastle won the return 3-0 after extra time on 11th December. Newcastle had become the first team to win the competition twice but couldn't go for a hat trick after Texaco's sponsorship was withdrawn.

FACT 58

1976
THE ONLY LEAGUE CUP FINAL

In 1975-76 Newcastle reached the League Cup final for the first and only time.

Newcastle looked a good bet to win the competition the previous season but in the quarter final at home to Chester they were held to a goalless draw before losing the replay 1-0, meaning three of the four semi finalists would be from outside the top flight.

In the second round of the 1975-76 competition Newcastle made no mistake when drawn against lower division opposition, beating Southport 6-0 away from home with Alan Gowling scoring four goals. They then overcame a scare against Bristol Rovers, against whom they came from 1-0 down to snatch a 1-1 draw before winning the replay 2-0 at St James' Park.

After beating Queens Park Rangers 3-1 away in the fourth round, Newcastle avoided another slip up against Second Division Notts County in the quarter final, winning a home tie 1-0.

In the semi final against Tottenham, Newcastle lost the first leg 1-0 at White Hart Lane, but in the return leg Gowling cancelled out the deficit in the third minute. Further goals in the second half from Glenn Keeley and Geoff Nulty booked Newcastle's Wembley place.

In the final against Manchester City Peter Barnes scored in the eleventh minute, but Gowling equalised midway through the first half. However after the break an overhead kick by Dennis Tueart won the cup for City and the nearest Newcastle have been to the final since was in 2006-07 when they reached the last eight.

FACT 59

1976 THROWN OUT OF THE ANGLO-SCOTTISH CUP

Whereas fielding weakened teams in the cups may seem normal today, in 1976 it got Newcastle United thrown out of a competition.

The Anglo-Scottish Cup was inaugurated in 1975-76 to replace the Texaco Cup, but was open to teams from England and Scotland only. Newcastle entered in its first year but failed to get out of a group that also included Carlisle, Middlesbrough and Sunderland, the same three teams they were drawn against in the Texaco Cup the previous season.

In 1976-77, Newcastle overcame Hull, Middlesbrough and Sheffield United to top their group, with all of these games being played pre season and providing a useful warm up exercise. For the first leg of the quarter final away to Ayr United on 15th September however, midfielder Tommy Craig was the only player in the starting eleven who had also played against Manchester United the previous Saturday.

Ayr dominated the game and could have won by more than the 3-0 scoreline, but Newcastle were denied the chance to overturn the deficit in the second leg as they were expelled from the competition. It was the last time they would take part, although it would go on for another four seasons.

FACT 60

1977
TEN STRAIGHT DEFEATS LEADS TO RELEGATION

Newcastle's worst ever run came in 1977-78 when ten straight defeats near the start of the season set them on the road to relegation.

The previous season first team coach Richard Dinnis took over as manager after Gordon Lee was sacked and he led Newcastle into the UEFA Cup, so the bad start to the new season was a big surprise. On the opening day Newcastle beat Leeds 3-2 at St James' Park but then had a run of ten straight defeats, with the team failing to score in four of the first five of those.

The run was finally ended with a 1-0 win at home to Chelsea on 22nd October and although the next two games, against Everton and Arsenal, were drawn, a 3-1 home defeat to Bastia that meant UEFA Cup elimination meant Dinnis was sacked.

Newcastle were bottom of the First Division and amidst a grip of player power, so the appointment of disciplinarian Bill McGarry was seen as a much needed move. He briefly arrested the slide, leading Newcastle to three successive wins in December and lifting them to third bottom, but that was as good as it got.

On Boxing Day Newcastle lost 4-0 at Manchester City and the 2-0 win at Leeds on 2nd January was their last of the season, as they failed to win any of their last nineteen games. Relegation was confirmed with a 2-0 defeat at Aston Villa on 17th April, meaning they were down with three games left to play.

The points total of 22 was Newcastle's lowest ever but McGarry was given a chance to turn things around. However after two mid table seasons in the Second Division he was sacked early in 1980-81 after a League Cup defeat to Third Division Bury.

FACT 61

1979 RECORD LOWEST ATTENDANCE

The lowest recorded league crowd at St James' Park came at the end of 1978-79 when just 7,134 turned out to see Newcastle United face Wrexham.

After being in with a chance of promotion at Christmas five straight defeats ended Newcastle's hopes, the low point being at the end of February when they lost 4-1 at home to Sunderland.

Crowds gradually dropped and this match, the last of the season, came after a 3-1 home defeat to Brighton three days earlier that left Newcastle in eleventh place. It was the second time Wrexham had came to St James' Park that season, as the first game at the end of March had to be abandoned at half time due to atrocious weather conditions.

Despite the eerie atmosphere it was an entertaining game, in which Alan Shoulder gave Newcastle a sixth minute lead. Ironically, Shoulder had played against Wrexham at St James' Park the previous season in front of over 42,000 fans. On that occasion the ground was hosting Northern League side Blyth Spartans' FA Cup fifth round replay against the Welsh side.

Newcastle's second came after 52 minutes through Jim Pearson and although Wrexham had played the night before against Luton they still put up a spirited display in this game.

There has never been a lower crowd for league games since, although in 1992-93 just 4,609 turned out for an Anglo-Italian Cup game against Cesena.

FACT 62

1980
LOCAL BREWERY IS FIRST SPONSOR

For the 1980-81 season Newcastle United had a shirt sponsor for the first time which led to the famous blue star logo being emblazoned across the front.

Hibernian in Scotland were the first British club to display a shirt sponsor in 1978, then in 1979-80 Liverpool became the first English club to do so. For 1980-81 many more clubs followed, with Scottish & Newcastle Breweries sponsoring Newcastle and displaying the famous blue star of Newcastle Breweries (who had merged with Scottish Brewers in 1960) on the shirt. Television restrictions though meant that plain shirts had to be worn for televised games until 1983.

Scottish & Newcastle are one of eight shirt sponsorship deals Newcastle have had, although only three different types of product have been advertised - telecommunications and financial services being the others in addition to beer.

Another brewery, Greenalls, were sponsors from 1986 to 1990 before McEwans and Newcastle Blue Star, individual beers produced by Scottish & Newcastle, took over for periods of five years each for the next decade. Cable phone and television company NTL were the shirt sponsor between 2000 and 2003 then bank Northern Rock had the honour for eight years. In 2011 Virgin Money took over and in 2013, loans company Wonga was displayed on the shirts.

FACT 63

1982
KEEGAN SIGNS IN UNIQUE CROWD RELATED DEAL

In the summer of 1982 Newcastle United stunned the football world by signing ex European Footballer of the Year Kevin Keegan from Southampton, with his contract containing clauses relating to gate receipts.

There were plenty of clubs Keegan could have gone to, but he was attracted by how besotted manager Arthur Cox was with the game and his desire and enthusiasm to see Newcastle return to the top.

Keegan's contract at Southampton allowed for him to be sold for £100,000 but during the negotiations he was advised that crowds could double if he signed. As such both parties agreed that Keegan would have a 15% cut of any gate receipts above 15,000 on top of a basic wage. It meant profit for both sides and if crowds didn't rise, the club would not be burdened by having agreed to an extravagant wage.

Keegan's arrival became the catalyst for more signings such as his ex Liverpool teammate Terry McDermott, who returned to St James' Park seven years after leaving for Anfield.

For Keegan's first game against Queens Park Rangers 36,185 turned out and the final season's average was 24,510, some 7,000 higher than in 1981-82 and excellent considering Newcastle never looked like being promoted and gates across the country were falling.

FACT 64

1982
ST JAMES UNDERGROUND STATION OPENS

In 1982 St James' Park got its own underground station as the new metro line was extended to the stadium.

The Tyne and Wear Metro first opened in 1980 and is one of only three underground networks in the United Kingdom outside London, the others being in Glasgow and Liverpool.

St James station, situated just fifty metres from the Gallowgate end of the ground, opened on 14th November 1982, extending the yellow line from Tynemouth via North Shields and Wallsend. The first time that fans were able to make use of it was on 27th November, when Newcastle took on Cambridge United.

When the station first opened it was coloured cream and yellow, as were all others on the network. But it is now decked out in black and white as well as having images of the ground and former players and managers.

St James station became the nearest underground station in England to a football ground, slightly nearer than Arsenal station was to their old Highbury ground. It is also the only one named directly in relation to a ground, as in London, Upton Park reflects the name of the surrounding area rather than the home of West Ham United.

FACT 65

1984 NEWCASTLE PROMOTED AS KEEGAN RETIRES

In 1983-84 Newcastle won promotion back to the First Division after a six year absence, with Kevin Keegan scoring in his last competitive game.

Newcastle had made a promising start in 1982-83 but eventually slipped out of the promotion reckoning due to a lack of strength in depth. However a run of only one defeat in the last eight games that led to a fifth place finish showed that there was something to build on the following season.

Newcastle made a slow start but a nine game unbeaten run lifted them up to second by the middle of November. The introduction of Peter Beardsley to the side had been influential in this, while another new face, Glenn Roeder, a defender who could create attacks, also

made an impact after Christmas.

Over the course of the season Chelsea and Sheffield Wednesday pulled away at the top, leaving the last promotion place a straight fight between Newcastle and Manchester City. It eventually came down to the last day of the season, when 36,415 packed into St James' Park to see Newcastle win 3-1 against Brighton thanks to goals from Keegan, Beardsley and Chris Waddle.

Keegan was by now 33 years old and had announced his decision to quit playing in February. After promotion was secured, a friendly match was arranged with Liverpool five days later on 17th May, in which another capacity crowd witnesses him score in a 2-2 draw. After the game he left the ground in a helicopter, throwing his shirt onto the pitch from the air, but he would be back in another capacity in future.

FACT 66

1985 PETER BEARDSLEY'S DERBY HAT TRICK

In one of the most memorable derbies, Peter Beardsley scored a hat trick as Newcastle beat Sunderland 3-1 in 1984-85.

This New Year's Day match was eagerly awaited as it was the first league meeting since 1979-80 and the first in the top flight for eighteen years. Both sides were struggling with Newcastle having lost their last three games. Manager Jack Charlton, who took over after Arthur Cox quit following promotion, had a team selection headache with Chris Waddle & Glenn Roeder both injured.

The first half was played at a frenetic pace but its only goal was a cool one, Beardsley passing the ball into the net from the edge of the area after a poor clearance. Three minutes into the second half Howard Gayle brought down Wes Saunders in the area and Beardsley converted the penalty to make it 2-0. Sunderland's cause wasn't helped either as Gayle was sent off for dissent, having already been booked in the first half.

Beardsley had a chance to complete his hat trick when Newcastle were awarded another penalty after Kenny Wharton was brought down, but his kick was saved by Chris Turner. Sunderland pulled one back through Colin West and had a great chance for an equaliser when Barry Venison was clean through but Saunders made a last gasp challenge.

With ten minutes remaining Gary Megson laid the ball off to the unmarked Beardsley who slotted past Turner to complete his hat trick. It was the first Newcastle hat trick in the derby since Alex Tait's in a 6-2 drubbing of Sunderland in 1956. The next one came from Kevin Nolan in the 5-1 victory in 2010-11.

FACT 67

1987
LATE ESCAPE DOESN'T PREVENT BEARDSLEY FROM LEAVING

In 1987 Newcastle staged a late escape to avoid relegation to the Second Division but it wasn't enough to stop Peter Beardsley leaving in a record transfer deal.

The season began with a 2-0 defeat to Liverpool at St James' Park. Managed by Willie McFaul, Newcastle failed to win any of their first six fixtures. A 1-0 home victory in their seventh game against Wimbledon lifted them to nineteenth but by mid November they were bottom. A run of eight defeats and a draw left Newcastle six points from safety at the end of February.

A revival was sparked with a 2-1 home win over second bottom Aston Villa, the first of nine games undefeated. A 3-0 loss at eventual champions Everton followed but Newcastle didn't dwell on this, beating Chelsea and drawing at West Ham to secure their top flight status with two games to go. It had seemed improbable two months earlier, especially as the team finishing fourth bottom had to go into the play offs to avoid relegation.

The campaign had been an extremely disappointing one for Beardsley who managed just five league goals compared to nineteen the previous season. Having starred for England in the 1986 World Cup, he was much sought after and even though Newcastle avoided the drop, he couldn't be persuaded to stay.

Beardsley began pre season training with Newcastle for the next campaign but within days he was on his way to Liverpool for a new British record fee of £1.9 million. However he returned to St James' Park in 1993, having also gone played for Everton and enjoyed five more good years at the club.

1988

FACT 68 PAUL GASCOIGNE SOLD FOR A RECORD FEE

In 1987-88 Paul Gascoigne won the Young Player of the Year award before being sold for a British record fee.

Known as 'Gazza' he joined Newcastle as a school boy in 1980 and was captain of the 1984-85 FA Youth Cup winning side. That season he also made his first team debut as a substitute.

His first start was against Southampton on the opening day of the 1985-86 season in which he made 31 league appearances, scoring nine goals. His return over the next two seasons wasn't as good but he made up for this with his vision and appetite for the game, creating numerous chances for others.

In 1987-88 although new manager Jim Smith had led Newcastle to eighth in the table, their highest finish since promotion in 1984, he expressed his desire to leave.

With Champions Liverpool, Gascoigne's preferred destination, not being interested, it came down to a choice between Manchester United and Tottenham. Alex Ferguson believed he had secured Gascoigne's signature and went on holiday, only for the player to change his mind.

Tottenham's £2 million fee broke the record set by Beardsley a year earlier, although later that summer Tony Cottee joined Everton from West Ham for £2.3 million.

In September '88 Gascoigne made his England debut and is best remembered for his performances and tears following a yellow card in the 1990 World Cup that would have ruled him out of the final had England got there.

However his off the field problems meant he never fulfilled his potential for both club and country.

FACT 69

1988 ADOPTION OF THE CURRENT CREST

Newcastle United's current crest has only been in use since 1988 and draws upon the city's coat of arms, links with the sea and club colours for its inspiration.

In FA Cup finals of the 1950's Newcastle had often used the city's coat of arms on their shirts, then between 1969 and 1976 they used the city's coat of arms. From 1976 to 1983 a design of a magpie standing in front of the River Tyne and castle was used, then until 1988 there was a much more simpler crest, containing the letters NUFC and a magpie.

The crest that has been adopted since 1988 is very similar to that of the city containing a Norman castle, two seahorses representing the links with the sea and a lion holding a flag.

There are differences however. In the shield, rather than three small castles, there are black and white stripes instead and underneath this it simply says 'Newcastle United' rather than the Latin logo that translates as 'triumphing by brave defence.' Also the flag held by the lion is not the St George's flag that is on the coat of arms, but instead a blue cross on a red background.

FACT 70

1989 RELEGATION AS BIG SIGNING FAILS TO DELIVER

Relegation to the Second Division occurred in 1988-89 after Brazilian Mirandinha failed to live up to initial expectations.

Mirandinha, full name Francisco Ernandi Lima da Silva, was signed from Palmeiras in 1987 for £575,000. He was the first Brazilian to play in England. Despite showing flashes of individual brilliance, his form was inconsistent and he struggled with the far quicker pace.

In his first season he still scored a respectable eleven league goals from 26 appearances as Newcastle finished eighth. In 1988-89 he struggled as Newcastle failed to deal with the departure of Paul Gascoigne. They won only one of their first seven games, a surprise 2-1 win at Champions Liverpool. This was followed by a 3-0 home defeat to Coventry Willie McFaul was sacked.

Colin Suggett was caretaker manager until Jim Smith took over in December when Newcastle were bottom of the table. He inspired an initial revival with two wins out of three, the second a 2-1 win at Sheffield Wednesday on Boxing Day lifting them out of the relegation zone. This was followed though by four successive defeats that left Newcastle six points from safety before a run of one defeat in seven games hauled them up to within a point of staying up at the end of March.

However, successive losses against fellow relegation candidates Sheffield Wednesday, Southampton and Aston Villa were a serious setback. Relegation was confirmed in the third from last game, when West Ham, who were in even worse trouble than Newcastle, won 2-1 at St James' Park. Newcastle finished the season bottom of the table with just 31 points, nine adrift of safety.

FACT 71

1991
PENALTY DEFEAT AFTER 6-6 DRAW

One of the most amazing games Newcastle have ever taken part in was the 6-6 draw at Tranmere in the 1991-92 Zenith Data Systems Cup.

This first round tie of a competition that ran from 1985 to 1992 for clubs in the top two divisions was played on 1st October. It was Newcastle's second visit of the season to Prenton Park, having lost in the league 3-2 the previous month.

Lee Clark's shot was deflected into the net by Mick Quinn to give Newcastle the lead but they were soon 2-1 down, only for Quinn to equalise before half time. In the second half Gavin Peacock put Newcastle in front again then Tranmere hit back and it finished 3-3 after ninety minutes.

Tranmere went 5-3 ahead in extra time with two goals in two minutes, but Clark got one back in the first period then set up Peacock for the equaliser after the break.

In the last minute, Alan Neilson was brought down in the area and Quinn scored the penalty to complete his hat trick and make it 6-5 but it still wasn't over. Newcastle conceded a penalty which was converted by John Aldridge to complete a hat trick of his own and take the match to a shoot out. Newcastle went on to lose 3-2 with Quinn hitting the post and Clark and Liam O'Brien having their kicks saved.

Despite Newcastle's disappointment, it had been a brilliant advert for football in one of the first games to be televised on Sky TV, a year before they started showing Premiership games.

The 6-6 draw was one of only three occasions in English football when a match has ended with that scoreline, the other times being Leicester v Arsenal in 1930 and Middlesbrough v Charlton in 1960.

FACT 72

1991
SIR JOHN HALL ARRIVES

In late 1991 North East businessman John Hall took over Newcastle United and successfully set about transforming the club into a major force in English football.

The son of a miner, Hall was born in Ashington in 1933 and made his fortune in property development, with the Metro Centre in Gateshead in the 1980s being his most high profile scheme.

In 1991 with Newcastle close to administration he bought the club and installed Freddie Fletcher as Chief Executive, as well as giving positions to Freddy Shepherd and son Douglas Hall.

Sir John had a vision of creating a sporting empire in Tyneside and often used the term 'Geordie Nation'. However despite acquiring control of the Newcastle Falcons rugby union club, Newcastle Eagles basketball club and Durham Wasps ice hockey club (who were moved to Newcastle and re-named Newcastle Cobras) he would concentrate solely on football.

During his chairmanship Newcastle rose from the brink of relegation to the third tier to become serious challengers for the Premiership title and St James' Park was transformed into a modern arena.

In 1997 as he sought to retire from active involvement, Sir John handed over the chairmanship to Freddy Shepherd and passed his shareholding to his son Douglas. The Hall family's involvement in the club came to an end in 2007 when Mike Ashley bought them out.

FACT **73**

1992
KEEGAN SAVES NEWCASTLE FROM RELEGATION

In 1991-92 Newcastle looked in grave danger of falling into the third Division prior to the arrival of Kevin Keegan as manager.

Under the management of Osvaldo Ardiles, the team played an attacking style but this left them exposed at the back, as the 6-6 draw at Tranmere in the Zenith Data Systems Cup demonstrated. They won only one of their first eleven games and sank to the bottom of the table after a 3-1 defeat at Portsmouth on 5th October.

They recovered and climbed to fifteenth at the end of November but a disastrous run in the next two months left them entrenched in the relegation zone. Ardiles, who won only eight out of 41 league games in charge, was dismissed after a 5-2 defeat at Oxford on 2nd February, which left the club four points from safety.

Freddie Fletcher persuaded Keegan to return as manager after eight years out of football. 29,000 attended his first game in charge at home to Bristol City, nearly double that of the previous home match. Newcastle won 3-0 and a run of just two defeats out of eight games followed, a 1-0 win over Sunderland on 24th March lifting them to seventeenth out of 24 teams.

In April though, Newcastle lost five games in succession which saw them drop into the relegation zone with two games to go. A 3-1 victory over Portsmouth in the season's last home game lifted Newcastle to twentieth.

However there were still three teams with a chance of overhauling them. Their final game was away to Leicester who had a chance of promotion. Against the odds Newcastle won 2-1 at Filbert Street to stay up, allowing Middlesbrough to be promoted instead, and the following season would be unforgettable for all the right reasons.

FACT 74

1993 PROMOTION TO THE PREMIERSHIP

1992-93 saw promotion back to the top flight in a season that saw them enjoy their best ever winning sequence.

After avoiding relegation on the last day of the previous season, Newcastle started in great fashion, winning their opening eleven fixtures, a sequence that remains a club record. Only the fact that Charlton played an extra midweek fixture in the first week of the season kept them off the top until the middle of September but when they got there in their sixth game, they were never off it.

Before the season started Keegan signed Barry Venison and John Beresford to shore up a defence that leaked too many goals the season before and both were virtual ever presents in the side. Rob Lee was signed for £700,000 from Charlton in September and he played a vital role in midfield, creating attacks and getting forward to score ten goals himself.

The only blip came in January and February when there was a run of six games without a win, five of them being draws. They had built up such a lead though that they were still twelve points clear of third place Millwall.

Promotion and the title were secured in the third from last game on May Bank Holiday, a 2-0 win at Grimsby in front of 7,000 travelling fans. Andy Cole, who signed in March for £1,750,000 from Bristol City, got the first and the second came from leading scorer David Kelly, who finished the season on 25 goals.

Despite securing promotion there was no let up as Newcastle won their last two home games, the second a 7-1 thrashing of Leicester in which Cole scored a hat trick to fire a warning to the newly created Premiership of what was to come.

FACT 75

1993
COLE BRINGS GOALS TO NEWCASTLE

In Newcastle's first season in the Premiership Andy Cole broke the club's scoring record, hitting 41 in all competitions.

Cole's total overhauled the previous record set by George Robledo, who had scored 39 in 1951-52. Cole got 34 in forty Premiership appearances, one in the FA Cup and six in just three League Cup games.

It was a televised hat trick against Liverpool on 21st November, the first of two he would score in the league that season, which really brought him to national attention. Cole had already scored hat tricks against Notts County in both legs of a League Cup 2nd round tie and hit two against Oldham in Newcastle's previous league game. Liverpool though were by far the most high profile visitors to St James' Park to date that season and had picked up ten points from their last four games.

On a snowy Sunday afternoon Cole struck all his goals in the first half. The first saw him beat Bruce Grobbelaar to a low cross and the second came when Scott Sellars crossed and Cole got between Torben Piechnik and Neil Ruddock to score. Sellars again provided the third, with Cole side-footing the ball home.

The hat trick took his running total of goals to 21 and he got another treble in a 4-0 win over Coventry the following February. Cole went on to equal Robledo's record when he scored in a 2-0 win over Liverpool at Anfield on 16th April 1994, then beat it eleven days later with a goal in a 5-1 home win over Aston Villa.

FACT 76

1994 HIGHEST LEAGUE FINISH SINCE 1927

Newcastle's first season in the Premiership saw them finish in third place, their highest league position since they were Champions in 1926-27.

The first game back in the top flight ended in disappointment when Tottenham won 1-0 at St James' Park and this was followed by a 2-1 defeat at Coventry. But an encouraging 1-1 draw at Champions Manchester United followed and the 3-0 win over Liverpool in November was part of a four match winning run that took them to fourth in the table.

When Newcastle won 2-1 at Queens Park Rangers on 16th January a second place finish looked a real possibility as they were only three points behind Blackburn, but Manchester United were running away at the top, holding a thirteen point lead. A disappointing three match losing run followed, which included a 1-0 defeat at Blackburn but Newcastle responded by winning their next six matches. During this sequence they hit four goals on three occasions, which included a 7-1 thrashing of Swindon at St James' Park.

In the last match of the season Newcastle were at home to fourth place Arsenal, knowing that anything other than a seven goal defeat would guarantee a third place finish. Goals from Andy Cole and Peter Beardsley gave Newcastle won 3-0, meaning that they finished six points ahead of Arsenal and seven behind Blackburn.

During the season Newcastle scored 82 goals, more than any other team in the Premiership and fully justifying their media nickname of 'The Entertainers.'

FACT 77

1995 TRANSFER LEADS TO NEW FUNCTION SUITE

The £6 million transfer of Les Ferdinand from Queens Park Rangers in the summer of 1995 saw a handsome profit for his first club.

Newcastle had tried to sign Ferdinand, nicknamed 'Sir Les' by fans, in 1993 but QPR turned down the offer. When he did arrive though, a sell on clause meant his first club, non league Hayes pocketed £600,000 which allowed them to build a new function suite which was named in his honour.

Ferdinand scored on his Newcastle debut at home to Coventry on 19th August 1995 and then got two more the following week at Bolton. Feeding off the service provided by Peter Beardsley, he got 25 league goals in 37 games in 1995-96 as Newcastle finished second in the league.

When Alan Shearer arrived in the summer of 1996, Ferdinand gave up the number 9 shirt and took number 10 for himself. Their partnership yielded 49 goals as Newcastle were runners up again, but as the club tried to balance the books, Ferdinand was deemed expendable and sold to Tottenham for £6 million the following summer.

The sale backfired as Shearer was ruled out for the first half of the season through injury and Newcastle struggled for goals. The club owners had initially tried to stop the transfer, but Ferdinand told them he was not prepared to let Spurs down once he had given them his word.

Ferdinand has remained well regarded on Tyneside and made a guest appearance for Newcastle in Shearer's testimonial in 2006.

FACT 78

1996 WORLD TRANSFER RECORD BROKEN

Eighteen months after the shock transfer of Andy Cole to Manchester United, Newcastle United made a clear statement of intent when they broke the world transfer record to sign Alan Shearer.

Cole had scored 68 goals in 85 appearances when he was sensationally sold to Manchester United in January 1995 for £7 million, a move that led to Kevin Keegan trying to justify the transfer to fans from the steps of St James' Park.

Cole upset fans by saying said he was joining a better club and when Newcastle surrendered a twelve point lead in the title race in 1995-96, Cole won his first title. That summer Gosforth born Alan Shearer, who had won the title with Blackburn the year before, was the top scorer in the European Championship with five goals and the race for his signature began.

Shearer held talks with Alex Ferguson and looked set to team up with Cole at Manchester United, but Blackburn were reluctant to sell to them. This opened the door for Keegan to make his approach and he was able to persuade Shearer that his future lay with Newcastle, but it needed a £15 million offer to secure the deal.

Shearer justified the fee in his first season, scoring 25 goals in 31 league games, meaning he was the Premiership's top scorer for the third season running. He was also named Professional Footballers' Association Player of the Year and would go on to enjoy nine more memorable seasons with Newcastle.

FACT 79

1996
NEWCASTLE THRASH THE CHAMPIONS

One of the greatest ever performances came on 20th October 1996 when Manchester United were hammered 5-0 at St James' Park.

After losing out in the title race to Manchester United in 1995-96, Newcastle started the new season well and the week before this game a 1-0 win at Derby, their seventh in nine games, took them top of the table.

Determined to also gain revenge for a 4-0 Charity Shield defeat at Wembley two months earlier, Newcastle went at the Champions from the start and took the lead after twelve minutes when Gavin Peacock headed in a corner. On the half hour David Ginola's unstoppable shot made it 2-0 and it remained that score at the break.

In the second half Newcastle knew sitting back wasn't the right way forward and just after the hour mark Alan Shearer crossed for Les Ferdinand to head the ball past Peter Schmeichel. With fifteen minutes remaining it was 4-0, Schmeichel making a double save from Peter Beardsley and Ferdinand before Shearer smashed the ball home.

The fifth goal was the best of the lot, as Rob Lee and David Batty combined to set up Belgian defender Philippe Albert, who exquisitely chipped Schmeichel from thirty yards.

Despite this victory Newcastle again faded in the title race, with Kevin Keegan resigning in January and being replaced by Kenny Dalglish. Although he shored up the defence and took Newcastle into the Champions League, such exhilarating attacking football didn't follow.

FACT 80

1997
NO SUNDERLAND FANS AT ST JAMES' PARK

In 1996-97 Newcastle United and Sunderland met in the top flight for the first time since 1985, but there were no away fans at either of the fixtures.

It was Sunderland's last season at their old Roker Park home, which still contained terracing whilst all other grounds were all seated. For the 4th September meeting there Sunderland announced that no Newcastle fans would be allowed to attend on safety and security grounds, but then compromised and said that 1,000 tickets would be allocated.

However by then arrangements had already been made for the game to be shown on giant screens at St James' Park and Newcastle rejected the offer, with Chief Executive Freddie Fletcher telling disappointing fans 'Don't blame Newcastle, don't blame Northumbria Police, blame Sunderland.' Despite having no fans in the ground it didn't stop Newcastle coming away with a result, as Peter Beardsley and Les Ferdinand scored in a 2-1 win.

For the return fixture the following April the ban was reciprocated, leading to pressure from fans towards both clubs asking for promises that this was not setting a precedent for future derbies. As with Newcastle at Roker Park, the lack of support did Sunderland no harm, as despite their position near the bottom they snatched a 1-1 draw.

All derbies since at both St James' Park and Sunderland's new home the Stadium of Light have been attended by 2-3,000 away fans.

FACT 81

1997 ASPRILLA DESTROYS BARCELONA

In Newcastle's first ever game in the Champions League, unpredictable Colombian Faustino Asprilla scored a hat trick as Barcelona were outclassed at St James' Park.

Asprilla had been dogged by inconsistency since his move from Parma in February 1996, but an injury to Alan Shearer early in 1997-98 gave him a chance to impress again.

Barcelona's side on 17th September 1997 included Rivaldo and Luis Figo but they were unable to get to grips with a buzzing St James' Park and rampant Asprilla, who was fouled early in the game by Michael Reiziger after he demonstrated his intentions.

Midway through the first half Asprilla was played through by Tomasson and he was brought down in the area by Barca keeper Ruud Hesp. The Colombian converted the penalty himself and just before the half hour mark he met Keith Gillespie's cross from the right with a thumping header to make it 2-0. Three minutes into the second half Asprilla again headed in a Gillespie cross and only the brilliant goalkeeping of Hesp denied him a fourth.

However Barca suddenly started playing and with seventeen minutes left Luis Enrique scored from close range and there were further scares for Newcastle when Rivaldo hit the bar from a free kick and had a great shot well saved by Shay Given. With a minute left Newcastle failed to clear a corner properly and Figo fired the ball home but they held on for the victory and one of St James' Park's greatest European nights.

For Newcastle and Asprilla though there would be no European glory. They finished third in the group and Asprilla never scored for them again before being sold back to Parma the following January.

FACT 82

1998
FA CUP GOALS RECORD BROKEN ON WAY TO FINAL

In 1997-98 Newcastle reached their first FA Cup final since 1974, with a long standing competition scoring record being broken in the third round.

Alan Shearer's ankle ligament injury sustained in pre season meant manager Kenny Daglish turned to Ian Rush, his old striking partner from Liverpool, to fill the gap. However at 36 Rush was now past his best and he didn't manage a league goal in fourteen appearances. His goal against Hull in the League Cup though took his total in the competition to 49, equalling Geoff Hurst's record.

In the FA Cup, Newcastle were drawn away to Everton in the third round, a game played on 4th January. In the second half, Rush came off the bench to score the only goal of the game, surpassing Denis Law's record of 42 goals. He only made two more appearances though as later that month Shearer returned to the side. Newcastle went on to beat Stevenage, Tranmere, Barnsley and Sheffield United to reach the final in which they were underdogs against league champions Arsenal.

Although Newcastle had beaten Arsenal in the two previous occasions they had faced them in an FA Cup final there would be no luck this time. Marc Overmars scored midway through a scrappy first half then after the break Shearer came close to equalising when he hit the post, then a Nikos Dabizas header hit the bar. In the 69th minute though Nicolas Anelka put the game out of reach, firing past Shay Given after springing the offside trap.

Arsenal's victory meant they had become only the second team to win the league and cup double twice, and they were sportingly applauded by the Newcastle fans as they collected the cup.

FACT 83

1999
UNLUCKY THIRTEEN AND FA CUP FINAL DEFEAT AGAIN

The Magpies reached the FA Cup final for the second season running in 1998-99 and again lost after finishing thirteenth in the league.

Dalglish, who had been unable to build on the second place finish of 1997 and whose style of football was in direct contrast to that of Keegan, was sacked after just two games of the season.

The new manager was Ruud Gullit, who had been inexplicably sacked by Chelsea the previous season while the club were second in the league and had reached the quarter finals of two cup competitions.

League results were inconsistent under Gullit and Newcastle again finished thirteenth in the league, but the FA Cup saw them see off Bradford, Crystal Palace, Blackburn and Everton to set up a semi final with Tottenham whose side contained ex Magpies players David Ginola and Les Ferdinand. At Old Trafford the score was 0-0 after ninety minutes but in extra time Alan Shearer scored a penalty in the first period after a Sol Campbell handball then got another with a minute remaining to book another trip to Wembley.

For the second year running Newcastle were up against the Premiership Champions in the final and they again lost 2-0 with the goals coming in each half. Teddy Sheringham scored Manchester United's first in the eleventh minute and the nearest Newcastle came to equalising before half time was when Dietmar Hamman's long range effort was saved by Peter Schmeichel. Gullit made an attacking change at half time, sending on Duncan Ferguson for Hamman but the game was beyond them from the 53rd minute when Paul Scholes made it 2-0.

FACT 84

1999 UNWANTED RECORD ENDED WITH 8-0 WIN

On 19th September 1999 Newcastle beat Sheffield Wednesday 8-0 to end a worst ever winless sequence of fourteen games.

Newcastle had failed to win any of their last seven games in 1998-99 and this disappointing run continued at the start of the new season, when they lost six and drew one of their opening seven matches. The fifth of these, a 2-1 home defeat to Sunderland for which Alan Shearer was dropped, led to the resignation of manager Ruud Gullit.

Gullit's assistant Steve Clarke took charge for the next game, a 5-1 defeat at Manchester United with Bobby Robson being appointed in time for the next game at Chelsea, which was lost 1-0. It meant his first game at St James' Park against Sheffield Wednesday, who were keeping Newcastle off the bottom on goal difference, was a crunch one.

Robson instilled a new confidence into his players and also re-instated Shearer to the side. It paid off as Aaron Hughes gave Newcastle an eleventh minute lead and Shearer struck a twelve minute hat trick to make the score 4-0 at half time.

A minute into the second half a brilliant solo goal from Kieron Dyer made it 5-0 but the sixth, from Gary Speed, didn't come until twelve minutes from time. Shearer then bagged his fourth before completing the rout from the penalty spot with seven minutes remaining. Robson continued to oversee improvement over the season as Newcastle lost twice in succession only once, eventually finishing eleventh. The 8-0 win remains their biggest in the Premiership era.

FACT 85

2000
ST JAMES' PARK RECONSTRUCTION

In 2000 the completion of a major expansion to St James' Park meant Newcastle United now had the second largest club ground in England.

Less than ten years earlier the ground was only covered on two sides with terracing at each end. In the mid 1990s a major refurbishment took place that led to an all covered and all seated capacity of 37,000. However this was nowhere near enough to satisfy demand and serious consideration was given to a move to a 55,000 capacity stadium in nearby Leaze's Park.

When plans for this were dropped in 1997 due to local opposition, it was decided to add extra tiers to two stands at St James' Park at the cost of £42 million.

Construction took place during 1999-00 and could be carried out without any reductions in capacity. New tiers were added to the Milburn and Leaze's stands, while in the East Stand (the oldest part of the ground) old executive boxes were removed and new rows of seating added. Many older seats were replaced and 1,000 were taken by Scottish side Elgin City and another 340 by local non-league club Blyth Spartans.

The new capacity was 52,143, meaning that St James' Park was now bigger than Sunderland's Stadium of Light which had opened in 1997 and only Manchester United's Old Trafford was bigger. Since then St James' Park has fallen to third in size with the construction of Arsenal's 60,000 seat Emirates Stadium, while changes since to the press box and adding seats in aisle areas have meant the capacity is now 52,387.

FACT 86

2001 THE FIRST PAY PER VIEW GAME

At the start of 2001-02 Newcastle made television football history when they were featured in the first pay per view game in the Premiership.

Pay per view was already a common feature for big boxing bouts and a small number of lower league games had been shown on this basis in the previous two seasons.

When it came to negotiating the new Premiership television deal that was to run from 2001 to 2004 it was agreed that Sky Sports would show forty games on a pay per view basis in addition to those that were available to subscribers.

Newcastle's match at Chelsea was the first to be selected for what was termed 'Premiership Plus', kicking off at 2pm on 19th August. After a ten minute delay caused by turnstile failures, Boudewijn Zenden gave Chelsea seventh minute lead but fourteen minutes from time Clarence Acuna equalised after Ed De Goey had failed to hold Laurent Robert's free kick.

The first pay per view game at St James' Park was on 30th September when Newcastle were beaten 2-0 by Liverpool. Premiership Pay per view games never proved as popular as anticipated and they were eventually dropped in 2007.

FACT 87

2001
AN EXTRA TIME HAT TRICK

In the second round of the League Cup in 2001-02 Craig Bellamy became the only Newcastle United player to score a hat trick in extra time.

Brentford shocked the St James' Park crowd when they took a seventeenth minute lead through Lloyd Owusu. They remained solid at the back and dangerous on the counter attack and it wasn't until just before the hour mark that Shola Ameobi equalised.

Newcastle had a great chance to win the game late on when Andy O'Brien had a header cleared off the line, but Brentford had their chances too and missed one good opportunity when Owusu fired wide.

During extra time Brentford were clearly tiring but they held out for the first period, with Alan Shearer's effort from a Nolberto Solano cross being well saved by the keeper.

In the 108th minute Bellamy finally ended Brentford's resistance when he cut inside from the left and hit a fierce shot past the keeper. Ten minutes later he added another and seconds before the end he completed his hat trick from close range, turning in a Solano cross.

FACT 88

2002 CHAMPIONS LEAGUE PROGRESS AFTER THREE DEFEATS

In the 2002-03 Champions League Newcastle lost their opening three group games but still progressed to the second phase.

After beating Bosnian side Željezničar in the qualifying round, Newcastle were paired in a tough group that included two former European champions as well as Dynamo Kiev, who had topped Newcastle's group in 1997-98. In their opening game Newcastle lost 2-0 in Kiev then a week later were beaten 1-0 at home by Feyenoord. A 2-0 defeat to Juventus in Turin followed but in the return fixture Andy Griffin scored the only goal at St James' Park.

A week after the Juventus game, Newcastle looked to be heading out when a goal early in the second half put Kiev 1-0 up, but Gary Speed equalised and then Alan Shearer converted a 68th minute penalty to give Newcastle the win. This set up a dramatic last matchday, with Juventus having qualified and all three other teams in the group still having a chance of joining them in the next phase.

In Rotterdam Newcastle scored twice in the first four minutes of the second half through Hugo Viana and Craig Bellamy to take control. However Dynamo Kiev then took a fiftieth minute lead against Juventus which put them in the driving seat. Juventus though hit back with two goals in eleven minutes, only for Newcastle to throw their lead away as Feyenoord fought back to 2-2 after 71 minutes. If the scores stayed like this, Kiev would qualify due to having a better head to head record but in injury time Bellamy struck a sensational winner to send Newcastle through.

It remains the only time a team has qualified for the next phase after losing their first three games. In the second group stage, Newcastle finished third in their groups behind Barcelona and Inter Milan.

FACT 89

2002
BRITISH FOOTBALL'S MOST EXPENSIVE TEENAGER

In June of 2002 Newcastle United signed Hugo Viana from Sporting Lisbon for £8.5 million, the highest fee involving a British club for a teenager.

Viana had been named Young European Footballer of the Year and was also a non playing squad member of the Portuguese national side that went to the World Cup that summer. His signature was a coup for Newcastle as Sporting had already agreed a fee with Spanish side Celta Vigo and Liverpool also made a late bid for the left sided midfielder.

The fee surpassed the £6 million that Coventry had received from Inter Milan for Robbie Keane in 1999, although it would be broken a year later when Sporting sold another teenager to an English club. Christiano Ronaldo, who went into their side after Viana had left joined Manchester United for £12 million.

Viana joined a Newcastle team that had a good blend of youth and experience and he scored one of the goals against Željezničar that took them into the group stages of the Champions League. However he failed to live up to expectations and he couldn't command a regular place in the side, with more than half of his forty Premiership appearances coming as a substitute.

In 2004 he returned to Sporting for a season long loan and for 2005-06 he went to Valencia, who paid £1.7 million to make his move permanent the following March.

FACT 90

2003 NEWCASTLE'S FASTEST GOAL

The fastest recorded goal in Newcastle United's history came on 18th January 2003 when Alan Shearer scored after just 10.4 seconds against Manchester City.

The match marked Kevin Keegan's first return to St James' Park as an opposition manager since he left in 1997 but his side couldn't have got off to a worse possible start. Just after kick off, former Newcastle player Steve Howey passed the ball back to their keeper Carlo Nash to give him an early touch. Nash though sliced his clearance straight into the path of Shearer who was closing him down, and the Newcastle striker gleefully rolled the ball into an empty net.

With Kieron Dyer and Jermaine Jenas dominating the midfield there was no way back for City, although Ali Bernabia did hit the post with a long range effort. After 65 minutes Craig Bellamy made it 2-0 to make the game safe for Newcastle.

The victory lifted Newcastle to third in the table, a position they maintained until the end of the season. Shearer's goal is the fastest known by any Newcastle player ever although there has been one quicker in the Premiership, when Ledley King struck after ten seconds flat for Tottenham against Bradford in 2000-01.

FACT 91

2004
RECORD NUMBER OF DRAWS IN A SEASON

In 2003-04 Newcastle United set a record for the most number of draws in a Premiership season.

Manager Sir Bobby Robson (who was knighted at the end of 2002) had led Newcastle to fourth and third place finishes in the last two seasons, but in 2003-04 they started badly. The team failed to win any of their first six games before four successive wins in October lifted them to seventh.

For the rest of the season Newcastle remained in the chase for a Champions League place and were fourth at the beginning of April. However their inability to put together a winning run was hindering them and between November and May they failed to win two successive games. They were partly distracted by a fantastic UEFA Cup run, which saw them reach the semi finals before losing 2-0 on aggregate to Marseille.

With three games to go Newcastle were fifth but Champions League qualification was in their own hands as their last game was away to fourth place Liverpool. However draws at home to Wolves and away to Southampton meant that the trip to Anfield counted for nothing and Newcastle had to settle for a UEFA Cup place.

The seventeen draws over the season set a new record for a 38 game Premiership season, which has since been equalled twice by Aston Villa, in 2006-07 and 2011-12.

In a move that angered many fans, Sir Bobby Robson was sacked early in 2004-05 after Newcastle failed to win any of their first four games.

FACT 92

2003
NEW TRAINING FACILITY OPENS

Three years after the completion of the re-structured St James' Park, Newcastle United's players also had a world class facility to train at when Darsley Park was opened.

Newcastle took out a 125 year lease on the old Civil Service sports ground in Benton, to the north of the city, to develop the new training centre. The purpose built facility opened in 2003 and is commonly known as Darsley Park although its official title is the Newcastle United Training Centre.

It contains a gymnasium and physio facilities, as well as a full size indoor pitch and all weather outdoor pitch, both of which use 'field turf' enabling training to take place in all conditions.

The venue has also been made available to the Newcastle Falcons rugby union team for training, with the Falcons having previously allowed Newcastle the use of their Kingston Park ground for reserve games.

Darsley Park is used for some reserve games while the club's academy is situated immediately south at Little Benton.

FACT 93

2005
MICHAEL OWEN ARRIVES IN NEW RECORD DEAL

The £15 million paid for Alan Shearer remained a club record for nine years until Michael Owen arrived in 2005, but this signing turned out to be arguably one of Newcastle United's biggest transfer mistakes.

The England striker had left Liverpool for Real Madrid a year earlier and although often a substitute he managed thirteen league goals, having the best ratio in terms of minutes on the pitch in La Liga. When Real signed Julio Baptista and Robinho in the summer of 2005 he became surplus to requirements, but his stock remained high and Newcastle had to pay £16.8 million to persuade him to come to St James' Park instead of return to Anfield.

There was naturally a great deal of excitement that Owen had chosen to come to Newcastle instead of a team that had just won the Champions League and 20,000 attended his unveiling. After being ruled out for the first month of the season with a thigh injury, he made a promising start with a goal in his second game, away to Blackburn and then got a hat trick at West Ham on 17th December.

However a broken metatarsal sustained against Spurs two weeks later was the start of a long line of injuries that would limit his appearances over the next three and a half years. The most serious of these was a cruciate ligament injury that occurred in the 2006 World Cup that kept him out for most of the next season and led to a long running compensation battle by Newcastle against FIFA.

His ratio of thirty goals in 79 appearances does not

look too bad, but that has to be considered against the fee paid and wages of over £100,000 a week. In 2009 he joined Manchester United after his contract expired, angering fans by saying he would rather sit on the bench at Old Trafford than be a first team player at Newcastle.

FACT 94

2006
SHEARER'S CAREER ENDS WITH GOAL AT SUNDERLAND

After ten years at Newcastle United, club record goalscorer Alan Shearer played his last match on 17th April 2006, scoring in a 4-1 win at Sunderland.

Shearer had repaid the world record £15 million fee many times over, scoring 206 goals in 405 appearances in all competitions, more than any other Newcastle player. This total may well have been even greater if he had not been injured for half of the 1997-98 and 2000-01 seasons.

Although his league total fell short of Jackie Milburn's, the 148 he did score for the club added to his Blackburn tally make him the Premiership's all time record scorer with 260. He was awarded the Freedom of the City of Newcastle upon Tyne in 2000 and the O.B.E. the following year.

Shearer initially intended to retire from playing in 2005 but was persuaded by manager Graeme Souness to give it another year, which led to him overtaking Milburn's record. In the game at Sunderland, he scored from the penalty spot to put Newcastle 2-1 up early in the second half but after 71 minutes he was forced to leave the field with an injured knee. Newcastle won the game 4-1, the biggest derby win since 1956.

The ligament damage sustained meant Shearer failed to recover by the end of the season and he was unable to play a full part in his testimonial the following month. However he was able to kick the game off and later came on as a substitute to score a penalty as Newcastle beat Celtic 3-2 in front of a capacity crowd at St James' Park.

FACT 95

2007
THE SHORTEST MANAGERIAL REIGN

After Glenn Roeder was sacked at the end of 2006-07 his replacement was a surprising choice and he ended up having the shortest spell in charge of any Newcastle United manager.

Sam Allardyce had no connections to the club, in fact he had even been a player with Sunderland at one stage of his career. Add to this his reputation for sending out teams to play a physical game without any free flowing passing, and it was not the appointment that fans wanted.

Newcastle had one of their best starts to the season for some time, losing only one of the first six games but the style of football wasn't what the fans were accustomed to. They then sank to mid table by the end of November, a month that included a disappointing 4-1 home defeat to Portsmouth.

There was further discontent in the League Cup, with Newcastle losing 2-0 to a second string Arsenal side. By the beginning of January with results and performances not improving Allardyce's position was becoming untenable, with hardly any fans backing him.

His spell in charge finally came to an end on 9th January 2008 following a meeting with owner Mike Ashley, who had been at the club since the previous summer. He had won seven and lost nine of the 21 Premiership games he was in charge for and he replaced Richard Dinnis as Newcastle's shortest serving manager, having overseen just 24 games in total.

FACT 96

2008 A HERO RETURNS

Following Sam Allardyce's spell in charge Newcastle United needed a manager that would excite the fans again, leading to the return of Kevin Keegan to St James' Park.

Keegan's return was a popular appointment but his reign began poorly. A capacity crowd that witnessed his first game against Bolton were subjected to a drab 0-0 draw and he failed to win any one of his first eight fixtures, which unluckily included games against Arsenal, Liverpool and Manchester United.

In the middle of March Newcastle were only four points off relegation but they then found their form and a 2-0 win over Sunderland on 20th April removed any lingering fears. It also extended Keegan's record over Sunderland to five wins in five games.

As 2008-09 began however there were signs of discontent as Keegan was unable to secure the funds from Mike Ashley to buy players he believed would improve the squad, in addition to reports that some players would be sold behind his back.

Newcastle began the new season with a 1-1 draw at Manchester United, but just three games in Keegan resigned, stating that a manager must have the right to manage and not have players imposed on him that he doesn't want.

Keegan's departure led to protests at the ground and a crowd of just 20,577 for a League Cup game with Tottenham, the lowest at St James' Park since returning to the top flight in 1993. It was just the beginning of what would be a disastrous season for the club.

FACT **97**

2009
SHEARER FAILS TO AVOID THE DROP

2008-09 turned out to be a disastrous one for Newcastle United as they got through five managers and ended up being relegated.

After Kevin Keegan's departure at the beginning of September 2008 Chris Hughton was caretaker for two weeks before Joe Kinnear, who had been out of football for four years, was appointed as interim manager at the end of the month. In November he was confirmed as manager until the end of the season but was forced to take break due to ill health in February when it was discovered he needed a heart bypass operation.

Hughton took over the role on a caretaker basis but after failing to win any of his five games in charge Alan

Shearer, by then working as a television pundit, agreed to take over for the last eight games of the season.

Shearer took over a side that had just slipped into the bottom three for the first time since October and he didn't have the easiest of starts at home to Chelsea, a game Newcastle lost 1-0. He didn't enjoy a win until his sixth game in charge, when a 3-1 victory over Middlesbrough at St James' Park lifted them out of the bottom three on goal difference.

The following week, Newcastle lost 1-0 at home to Fulham meaning that they had to better Hull's result on the last day of the season to survive. Even though Hull were beaten 1-0 at home by Manchester United, Newcastle lost 1-0 at Aston Villa bringing to an end sixteen years of Premiership football.

FACT 98

2010
NEWCASTLE STORM BACK TO THE PREMIERSHIP

After the pain of relegation in 2008-09, Newcastle United won promotion at the first attempt.

With Alan Shearer not being given the job on a permanent basis and Joe Kinnear unable to return due to ill health, coach Chris Hughton was again caretaker manager for the start of the season. However due to his excellent start, in which just one out of the first eleven games were lost and with Newcastle top of the league, the position was made permanent in October.

Between October and December Newcastle won seven games in a row for the first time since 1996. The unbeaten run stretched to fourteen games, but with five of the last seven being drawn they were unable to pull clear at the top and a 3-0 defeat at Derby on 9th February saw them drop to second, just three points clear of third place Nottingham Forest.

That Derby defeat was the last of the season as Newcastle then went their last seventeen games unbeaten. Promotion was secured on the afternoon of 5th April when Forest could only draw 0-0 with Cardiff, meaning there was a carnival atmosphere at St James' Park that evening as Newcastle took on Sheffield United knowing they were already promoted. Newcastle won that game 2-1 but didn't ease up in their last five games, winning four and drawing one with a 2-0 win at Plymouth confirming that they would go up as champions.

Newcastle's 102 points haul was a club record, while the crowd of 52,181 for the last game against Ipswich was a record for the Football League Championship since the Premiership was formed in 1992. Over the course of the season the average crowd was 43,383, the fourth highest in the country.

FACT 99

2011
THE PREMIERSHIP'S GREATEST COMEBACK

On 5th February 2011 Newcastle United came from 4-0 down to draw with Arsenal at St James' Park, the only time in the Premiership era that a team has managed to salvage something after being so far behind.

It was the first home game since supporters were disappointed to see Andy Carroll leave the club and their mood was made worse when Arsenal went 2-0 up in the first three minutes through Theo Walcott and Johan Djourou. Robin Van Persie made it 3-0 after ten minutes and got another in the 26th minute to make Newcastle's task look impossible. It could have been worse just before half time, with Newcastle keeper Steve Harper doing well to save a strike from Van Persie.

Five minutes into the second half Arsenal's Abou Diaby needlessly pushed Joey Barton to the floor before shoving Kevin Nolan and received a red card, but Newcastle couldn't make their numerical advantage count until the 68th minute when Barton scored a penalty. Seven minutes later Jose Enrique crossed for Leon Best to score and give the fans real hope, as by now Arsenal were reeling with a number of fouls being committed and Emmauel Eboue booked for dissent.

With seven minutes left Mike Williamson was fouled and Barton scored his second penalty of the game and the equaliser came with three minutes remaining, Cheik Tiote firing in from outside the area after Arsenal had failed to clear a free kick.

It led to wild celebrations from Newcastle fans after a difficult week and was also the first time since the formation of the Premiership in 1992 that a team had avoided defeat after being four goals down.

FACT 100

2012 FIRST MANAGER OF THE YEAR AWARDS

In 2011-12 Newcastle United finished fifth in the Premiership leading to manager Alan Pardew picking up two Manager of the Year awards.

Ex Charlton, West Ham and Southampton boss Pardew had been appointed manager in December 2010, when Chris Hughton was sacked despite a steady start to their first season back in the Premiership. Newcastle went on to finish in twelfth position, winning only five games in the second half of the season.

However in the summer Pardew made some shrewd signings including Yohan Cabaye and Sylvain Marveaux, while he also signed Demba Ba, who triggered a release clause in his West Ham contract allowing him to leave for free if they were relegated.

Newcastle enjoyed their best start to a Premiership season since 1994-95, remaining unbeaten for eleven games to go third in the table. A seven match winless run followed and Newcastle were seventh at the turn of the year, but in the transfer window Papiss Cisse arrived from Freiburg and his phenomenal goal return of thirteen goals in fourteen league games got Newcastle back on track.

Seven successive wins in March and April meant that Champions League qualification looked a real possibility, but this dream was ended after three defeats in the last four games. On the last day of the season though Newcastle had an outside chance of qualification, but a 3-1 defeat at Everton meant they had to settle for fifth.

Pardew's achievement was recognised by both the Premiership and League Managers' Association, who both voted him Manager of the Year. This was something that neither Kevin Keegan nor Sir Bobby Robson had managed to achieve.

Sources

www.toon1892.co.uk
http://www.nufctheyworethenewcastleshirt.btck.co.uk/

The 100 Facts Series

Arsenal, *Steve Horton*	978-1-908724-09-0
Aston Villa, *Steve Horton*	978-1-908724-92-2
Celtic, *Steve Horton*	978-1-908724-10-6
Chelsea, *Kristian Downer*	978-1-908724-11-3
Leeds, *Steve Horton*	978-1-908724-79-3
Liverpool, *Steve Horton*	978-1-908724-13-7
Manchester City, *Steve Horton*	978-1-908724-14-4
Manchester United, *Iain McCartney*	978-1-908724-15-1
Newcastle United, *Steve Horton*	978-1-908724-16-8
Norwich City, *Steve Horton*	978-1-908724-93-9
Rangers, *David Clayton*	978-1-908724-17-5
Tottenham Hostpur, *Steve Horton*	978-1-908724-18-2
West Ham, *Steve Horton*	978-1-908724-80-9

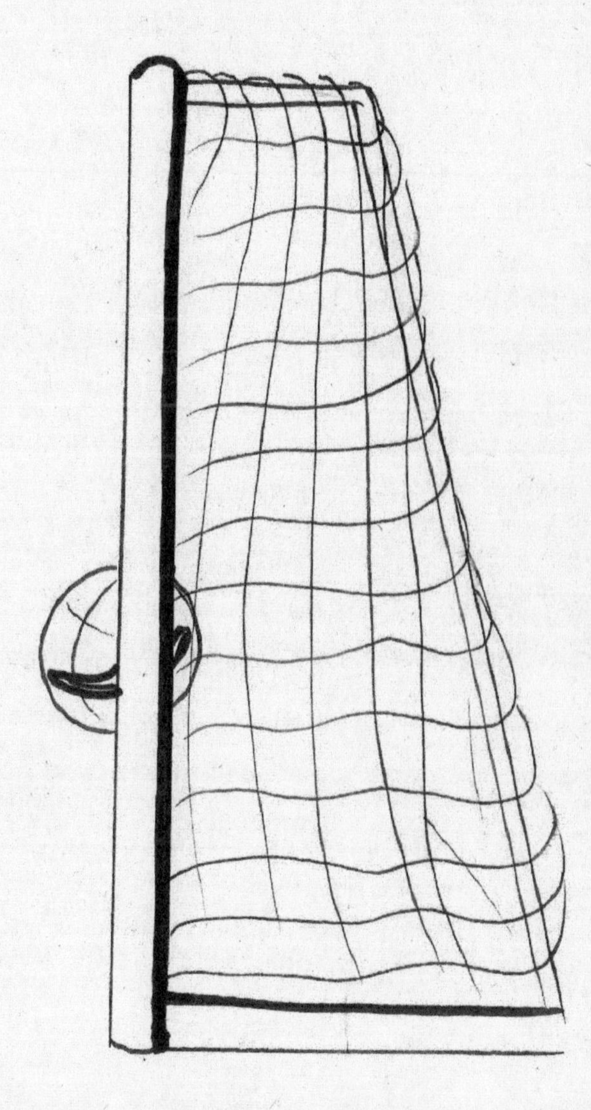